YOU LOOK GOOD FOR YOUR AGE

D1236000

YOU LOOK GOOD

RONA ALTROWS *Editor*

FOR YOUR AGE

An Anthology

UNIVERSITY
of **ALBERTA**
PRESS

Published by

University of Alberta Press
1–16 Rutherford Library South
11204 89 Avenue NW
Edmonton, Alberta, Canada T6G 2J4
uap.ualberta.ca

LIBRARY AND ARCHIVES CANADA
CATALOGUING IN PUBLICATION

Title: You look good for your age : an
anthology / Rona Altrows, editor.
Names: Altrows, Rona, 1948– editor.
Series: Robert Kroetsch series.
Description: Series statement: Robert
Kroetsch series
Identifiers: Canadiana (print) 20200324667 |
Canadiana (ebook) 20200324721 |
ISBN 9781772125320 (softcover) |
ISBN 9781772125733 (PDF)
Subjects: LCSH: Aging in literature. | LCSH:
Older women in literature. | LCSH:
Women in literature. | CSH: Canadian
literature (English)—Women authors. |
CSH: Canadian literature (English)—21st
century.
Classification: LCC PS8235.W6 Y68 2021 |
DDC C810.8/035246—dc23

First edition, first printing, 2021.
First printed and bound in Canada by
Houghton Boston Printers, Saskatoon,
Saskatchewan.
Copyediting and proofreading by
Meaghan Craven.

A volume in the Robert Kroetsch Series.

University of Alberta Press is committed to
protecting our natural environment. As part
of our efforts, this book is printed on Enviro
Paper: it contains 100% post-consumer
recycled fibres and is acid- and chlorine-free.

University of Alberta Press gratefully
acknowledges the support received for its
publishing program from the Government
of Canada, the Canada Council for the Arts,
and the Government of Alberta through the
Alberta Media Fund.

This work is published with the assistance
of the Western Canadiana Publications
Endowment.

For my contributors

Contents

ELDERS

BODY

LOVE

TIMELINES

ENOUGH!

Preface

THIS IS A BOOK about women, aging, and ageism. There are twenty-nine contributing writers, and we range in age from our nineties down to our forties. We all identify as female.

The idea for the book arose from my own life. In September 2018, I was diagnosed with obstructive sleep apnea and it was recommended that I get fitted for a device. A young respiratory therapist, seeing me for the first time, looked at my medical chart, which of course included date of birth, then scrutinized my face. "You look good for your age," she said. Inwardly, I was angry. But why? I mulled over my internal reaction for a while and figured out that the respiratory therapist's clichéd comment, while intended as a compliment, carried with it the social assumption that it is better to look young than old and, by logical extension, better to *be* young than old. Otherwise, the qualifier "for your age" would not be necessary.

Why are these assumptions made? What effects do they have on aging women? What messages about the aging process do we pass on to our daughters? Are those messages healthy? Or, as an aging woman, am I simply not willing to face up to the fact that when I see myself in the mirror, I am less satisfied than I used to be? And am I ashamed of feeling that way?

The questions just kept coming. And it struck me that I was not the only one asking them. So many women have aging on their minds. How can we not? The older we get, the more we find ourselves surrounded by ageist messaging, ghosted, relegated to invisibleness. In fact, women start having to deal with issues related to aging and ageism as early as in our forties.

It seemed to me the best way to explore those questions, and other questions I might well not have thought of, was to put together an anthology. So I invited some other professional writers who identify as female to send me their thoughts, using whatever creative forms they wished. Send they did, beautiful pieces with so many distinct views, impressions, and speculations on aging and ageism and their own growth as people.

This is our book. Serious, whimsical, satirical, angry, and impressionistic works all have a place in *You Look Good for Your Age*. The book contains the work of writers from varying backgrounds. Some come from communities involved in historical—and, unfortunately, current—fights for human rights: queer, Métis, immigrant, Jewish. Some struggle with mental health challenges such as anxiety, depression, panic disorder. What we all share is a belief in the essential value of women, the aging process, mutual respect.

The book is organized in thematic parts, there is a lot of overlap in themes, and each piece deals with multiple matters. We do not claim to cover every aspect of aging and ageism. These are takes on the subject. Since life imitates art imitates life *ad infinitum*, we have made it clear which prose pieces are fiction and which are nonfiction. Poetry also occupies an important place.

In INSIGHT, writers deal with vision versus eyesight, a changing approach to fear, the age-irrelevancy of meditation, the intent to forgive, the poetic possibilities of an empty nest, a floral perspective on the self.

ELDERS explores a daughter's parenting of parents with dementia, a daughter's learnings from a nonagenarian mother who continues to pursue her love of nature, a daughter's thoughts on the fierce love and complexity of a mother who has just died, an imagined social media page, a poet's recollections of the older women in her family, as experienced by her in adolescence.

BODY invites us to consider anti-aging Internet ads, the mature woman's care and treatment of hemorrhoids, the psychological benefits and perils of life in the gym, the aging woman's changing relationship with blood.

LOVE explores a married woman's affair that surprises the woman herself, the maddening proximity of an unattainable love, the fear of imminent loss of a long-time love, the convoluted path from alienation to self-love.

TIMELINES takes us to reflections and stories about the present and past self, the self and younger women, the shattered promise of a good life in a new town, the pain of losing a cherished friend. A woman in her forties looks at how she got to where she is; a woman in her fifties gazes forward and back, back and forward. A poet rejoices in the joys of dressing for comfort and reassuring smells.

We end the book with ENOUGH! In this part, writers deal with some common assumptions about women and aging (we should be infinitely patient, we should have grandchildren, we should shut up, et cetera) and say what they think about those assumptions.

Intergenerational sparring seems more common than ever now, as is illustrated by the insulting meme "Okay, boomer." But we are at a point in the history of our planet when it is critical that we take care of one another and cooperate in the work to be done, regardless of when we were born. So we invite readers of all ages and stages of life and everywhere on or off the gender spectrum. *You Look Good for Your Age* is for thinking, feeling people, period.

This afternoon, I returned to the same respiratory therapist for my annual checkup. I told her that her words to me, "You look good for your age," had inspired a book.

"Wow!" she said. "You wrote a whole book about that?"

"Twenty-nine kick-ass writers wrote it," I said.

She gave me a thumbs up.

RONA ALTROWS
Calgary, Alberta

Acknowledgements

IT'S ALWAYS A PLEASURE to work with the folks at University of Alberta Press. I'm grateful to Director Doug Hildebrand and Associate Director Cathie Crooks for their belief in the project and in my ability to pull it off, even when I was not so sure I could. Big thanks to Acquisitions Editor Mat Buntin, who worked closely with me as the manuscript took shape. Mat answered my frequent, numerous questions with full information, invariable patience, and when called for, sly humour. Thanks to Alan Brownoff for yet another great book design. Thanks to Production Editor Duncan Turner for his good eye. Thanks to Meaghan Craven for a thorough, thoughtful copyedit.

This book would not be a proper whole without the participation of every contributing writer. Your works speak for themselves. Thank you all so much.

Thank you to Sharon Butala, Aritha van Herk, Merna Summers, Debbie Bateman, Wendy McGrath, Jane Cawthorne, and JoAnn McCaig, for sending me encouraging words about the project and my own ability when, as it turned out, I most needed to hear those words.

For help in various ways, thanks to Peter Midgley, Alice Major, Bill Paterson, Lucy Altrows, Grace Paterson, Judy Gray, Red Davis, Barbara Buntin, and Gerry Kelley.

A grant from the Alberta Foundation for the Arts made it possible for me to pay the contributing writers well, something I feel strongly about. Thank you, AFA.

And special thanks to respiratory therapist Miranda Liu, for the casual comment that sparked the idea for this book.

INSIGHT

The Fixable

SHARON BUTALA

SOME MONTHS AGO, during a close examination of my eyes, a young optometrist told me that I had macular degeneration "just barely starting" in both of them. She stood with her back to me, fiddling with something, speaking in a low, light voice that signified to me that either she wasn't sure if she should tell me or not, or wasn't sure how to tell me. Maybe I was the first person she had ever had to give such bad news. I paid her no mind, it being clear to me that I would somehow escape this verdict, or, because I was then almost seventy-eight years old, before the condition took full effect I would be dead. Case closed, as they say on TV.

I left her examination room as jauntily as I had entered it, even though I had been having trouble with my right eye ever since my cataract surgery four years earlier and there seemed to be no explanation for it. I couldn't rub away the haze, or wash it out of my eye or off the lens of my glasses, or blink it away, and to be truthful, I sometimes missed letters in words when I was reading and had to go back to where, miraculously, the missing letter or letters would reappear. Sometimes I would see things or people at the edge of my vision when there was no one or nothing there, all of which

I had told the optometrist, which is what had caused her to do the deeper examination resulting in her, I thought, faintly weird behaviour as she made the pronouncement of macular degeneration.

For at least a full month her diagnosis seemed to me distant and unreal, ignorable because it wouldn't come to pass during my lifetime. I was still vigorous and often told I was unusually young-looking for my age. I was also still stubbornly working as a writer, still publishing, even though small voices in my head were whispering to me that I was done, that my time as a writer had passed, that I no longer understood the world and anything relevant I might have to say was relevant only to us, the nearly dead (my occasional, not entirely whimsical term for my age group—people approaching eighty and over). I knew people with MS, or COPD, or Parkinson's disease, or the beginnings of some kind of dementia, many of them younger than me, so clearly, I thought, it wasn't my fate to be hit with that kind of catastrophe. That I even had these thoughts was evidence, although I ignored that too, that the optometrist's diagnosis was working away below my full consciousness.

I mentioned this verdict to an acquaintance—odd that I would choose to tell her and not my family—who lent me a twenty-year-old book on the subject written by an ophthalmologist who, in middle age, had developed the problem himself. By the time I had finished his book it began to sink in (or so I thought then), that I had to accept I was facing the end of my life as I knew it. My next thought was to look around for help, somebody to tell this to. But it was summer and most of my close friends were off on vacations, and not many months before, my family had moved a couple of thousand miles away, and anyway, I thought it far too soon to burden them with this news. I was alone and could think of no one I wanted to phone to talk with about the fact that I was about to go blind and at a time when I was already old and losing abilities and continuously wondering who would care for me when I could no longer care for myself, and surreptitiously considering available options, as were the number of single, aging women (from early sixties to over ninety) with whom I was acquainted. All of us, as we talked about the problem facing us, which was where we would end our lives, trying not to sigh audibly, gazing absently out the window, our expressions carefully neutral.

Already, as with many old people, I was having trouble filling my evenings and weekends in activities with my friends, a number of whom still had husbands or grown-up children and their families nearby and who reserved their own time for when their families weren't working or in school. And now, to be blind as well! I who had spent my life reading, studying, going to films, sometimes painting, and staring at a computer screen as I wrote book after book, more than twenty in all. How would I fill all those endless, solitary hours when I could not see? An unexpected rage engulfed me, and I spent an entire weekend lost in it, clomping down park pathways, trying to breathe through its heat, trying not to have my head explode while it churned with incoherent thoughts, on fire with indignation, and violent half-images that seared my brain and that I killed at once, only to have others appear before I mentally bashed them out of sight.

Here is where I explain—says she, bitterly—that not being able to see is actually quite a wonderful thing, and that friends and family will/would rally around and buy my groceries for me, and guide me on walks and take me to the symphony and chamber concerts. Here is where I explain that blindness is good for the soul as well. Hah! I could think of nothing worse—wait, of course I could, from severe debilitating chronic pain to dying in a dungeon for a crime you didn't commit. I suppose I meant that, in terms of who I am, within a "normal" North American life, I could think of nothing worse: To be completely alone to deal with this life-changing and inalterable verdict; to realize my working life as a writer after forty years was over, and I did not know what I would do in place of it; to realize that almost certainly I was not going to die before the full force of the condition hit; to know that I was caught in a vice of destiny's making, and I did not even have anybody to say this to. I mean, you don't tell it to the women you always see in the grocery store, or your-across-the-hall neighbour with whom you have a tenuous relationship at best, or the woman with whom you have lunch once a month. Although I had two sisters left, one was in Europe for the summer (even though in a wheelchair) with her family, and the other had a serious long-term illness, and in any case, both lived far away from me. As for my close friends, they had troubles of their own and didn't need to add mine to their burdens. (At least in this, I was honest. Sort of.)

One evening I noticed that the pill container I used when I travelled had the days of the week written on it in braille— at least, I assumed those little bumps, each set different, were braille—and was surprised and pleased. A glimmer of hope entered the blackness of my fury and near-despair. I had bought the container where I buy most of the things I need for my daily life, merely at the Co-Op down the street, and not in some specialized store for the blind. Okay, so I would have to learn braille. My head was clearing. I began to try to imagine how I would live with this disability, practically, step by step.

Occasionally, when I couldn't sleep, I tried to put on my bedside radio and find the CBC without turning on the light, running my fingers over the buttons, counting, trying to locate the right one. I closed my eyes, too, and concentrat on the meaningful sounds, a musical phrase, a few vowels anu consonants in different voices coming softly, intimately from the radio in the 3 AM hush. Or I searched for my glasses or my keys with my eyes closed, testing how well I could navigate without sight in my own home. Already a sightless world was closing in around me, and I saw how intimate it would be, how solitary, if, possibly and in some way, I wasn't yet sure about, how blessed. But I also could see myself growing more and more careless, showing up in my summer navy and white polka-dot pants with a plaid shirt, not the plain white one I thought I had on, my hair ravaged and unsightly, eventually throwing myself in front of a commuter train. Whoa!

I reminded myself over and over again that if I had macular degeneration, according to the ophthalmologist whose book I had read, I would always see light, would never be in total darkness. I thought of books I had read about the blind heroes: Helen Keller, Jacques Lusseyran, people whose breathtaking adaptability was interwoven with unquenchable bravery, and despite my anger, I was inspired by them. I knew damn well I didn't have their courage. I was already worn out with the endless uncertainty and never-ending troubles of being alive.

Not only did I not tell anyone for at least a month, possibly two, I didn't do anything about the diagnosis, at first thinking that nothing could be done anyway, so why bother, and also, I suspect that at a deep level, I still thought the problem would miraculously go away and I would be fine. Because she had been so careful and focused in her examination, I honestly don't think it occurred to me that my optometrist might simply be wrong, or if I did, this alone I attributed to wishful thinking. I kept telling myself that many, many old people have this condition and I wasn't in any way special and so should just shut up about it.

I consulted a friend who uses a white cane; I talked with an acquaintance with macular degeneration as well as other difficulties with her eyes. The first told me he could introduce me to the most wonderful people at the CNIB, praised them so highly I almost cancelled our lunch plans and went immediately to them. He promised me, too, that when the time came, he would show me the ropes of being legally blind. (Legal blindness occurs if your best eye has less than 20/200 vision when corrected with glasses or contacts. According to Alberta Health, 20/200 means "a person cannot be more than 20 feet away to see what a person with normal vision can see from 200 feet away.")

The other acquaintance commiserated, but not in an "Oh, you poor thing" way, but more a "Damn it all! It's a helluva thing" way (which I liked), and offered me a high-resolution reading tool she no longer used. I noted, too, that though neither of them saw well enough to drive, they both went about the city with what seemed to me to be freedom, even insouciance, by using taxis and services for the disabled, and sometimes relying on friends or family. I asked myself, is this perhaps doable after all? Finally, I bestirred myself enough to ask an ophthalmologist I knew if I should be taking some medicine or doing eye exercises or something to maybe ameliorate the progression of the condition. She told me to come and see her.

I got a referral. Convinced now that I had the disability and knowing that there was no cure, I had begun to try to be cheerful about my fate, or at least, to try to find a livable, decent approach to it. A part of me was holding off though. I could feel it; it was saying *wait, hold on*, the diagnosis isn't certain yet, you need to wait. In the soulful blackness of my interior, where I came to understandings and made firm decisions from which there would be no going back, I was still holding on, weightless, not daring to take too deep a breath. How I would handle it all would have to come when I knew for sure I was about to go legally blind.

Eventually I told my friends. The people I knew who were legally blind, having lived in Calgary all their lives, had networks of friends, or close family members nearby, or both. I had friends, mostly younger than I am and therefore busy already who didn't need another drain on their energy, and anyway, I hadn't known them for more than five years. I knew they couldn't hand over their lives to me, and I would have been ashamed if I had caught one of them trying to. The possibility of moving closer to my son and his family I quashed at once. At least I knew my way intimately around my own condo, my building, and my neighbourhood. My sisters would be unable to help me—one was in a wheelchair and the other in serious ill health—and even with malfunctioning sight, I would still be the healthy one. But at our ages it was touch and go as to who would be the first to depart. It would be crazy to uproot myself at this moment in my life, only to find myself, sooner rather than later, a stranger in a strange community, and blind.

Wait a minute, I told myself: you're jumping the gun; maybe your eyes are okay and all this emotional turmoil is over nothing. Hah! I said to myself, with my history of bad luck? Quit kidding yourself; of course you're going blind, and do not ever forget that so are thousands of other old people. Blindness is a commonplace as people grow old and then older again. And older after that. (A 2013 WHO report: "In 2010, 82% of those blind and 65% of those with moderate and severe blindness were older than 50 years of age.")

Such a diagnosis would be the end of people telling me how young I look for my years (a source of faintly surprised pride, I realized, no matter how much I pretended it wasn't), but that seemed hardly worth thinking about. When you're old, you're old; no matter what you look like, you are still in the last few years of your life: the last quarter, the last third, the last tenth. If there are maybe a few advantages to not looking your age—the occasional younger male hits on you—there are also disadvantages—the same younger male vanishes when he finds out you are twelve or fifteen years older than he is, if not older than that. I lost one boyfriend because (well, there might have been other reasons as well) I was four years older than he was. I guess he thought that by the time I was eighty-four and in total swamp-creature decrepitude, he would still be seventy and continuing to make out with fifty-year-olds. As an adult woman in our age-hating society, the younger you look, the less likely you'll be ignored or dismissed, which is an important advantage, but no guarantee of anything else.

The day of my ophthalmologist's appointment arrived. After about forty-five minutes of sitting in front of one machine and then another, blinking or not-blinking as requested, my vision blurry from drops, she told me I did not have macular degeneration. Then she went on to tell me that I had preconditions for glaucoma, which would require watching and possibly, in a year or two, actual treatment, and also, that she was going to refer me to a retina specialist as another condition she had discovered meant that I was in steady danger of having detached retinas. Oh, I said. I couldn't think of anything else to say. My entire brain had scrunched itself up into a puzzled, partially disbelieving—or maybe awed—frown.

The problems that had taken me to the optometrist in the first place were negligible and probably even fixable if I wanted to have a laser treatment or two. No thank you, I said. Better to let sleeping dogs lie, which, come to think of it, is what I say to my dentist, too, while crossing my fingers. (It's amazing to me how much I count on being dead before the real horrors get the chance to hit.) I saw that it was a good thing the optometrist had made a mistake because without her diagnosis, I would never have seen the ophthalmologist, which turned out to be, if for different reasons, crucial for my continuing ability to see. At first friends said, "Thank heavens," when I said I didn't have macular degeneration, but I pointed out, "Medicine can slow glaucoma, but it can make you completely blind." Completely blind: without perceptible light. "While there is no treatment for macular degeneration, at least you aren't in full darkness." Despite everything, there was some room for relief, or joy. I just don't see very well, to go along with not hearing very well or sleeping very well, and with having achy joints, and occasional memory glitches. Ah well, I thought, finally, drawing in my breath shakily, surrendering to the fact of the inevitable finally getting its claws into me.

The hardest lesson of growing old is to recognize finally that you aren't special, that fate will do with you whatever it wants, just as it does with everybody on this planet. First, even though I didn't look or act "old" at all, it made me old. Now I, too—wonderful me!—could go legally blind like anybody else and have to end my life using special aids, hiring people to assist me (if I could afford it), and spending most of my time alone in my condo listening to podcasts or whatever. Nothing special about that end; in our society, a commonplace, though also a tragedy. Aging Gloucester, savagely blinded by his enemies. Blind Homer, telling one of the greatest tales ever told, it lasting in written form for nearly three thousand years. Nor would I be dragging around the streets in rags, with my gnarled cane and my begging cup.

If you're lucky, as I am, this is how you get old: incrementally, your body wearing out bit by tiny bit, small wound by small wound, your soul wearing away with it all, thinning, loosening from its anchors, eternity coming closer every day.

Fearing

ARIEL GORDON

STANDING ON THE EDGE of the five-metre diving board. The pool deck is gritty beneath my bare feet, my skin and hair are thoroughly chlorinated, and I only have two options: jump or back down.

It's Sunday afternoon at the public pool and I'm working with fear.

My nine-year-old daughter is a few feet behind me, watching me closely. But I'm only peripherally aware of her: I'm in full fight-or-flight mode. My belly is clenched, my knees are shaking, and my brain is nattering at me: What am I doing? Why would *anyone* want to jump from this height? I'll hurt myself! That water will be like concrete!

I jump.

This isn't my first Sunday afternoon. Last time, I conquered the three-metre board.

The trick, I've discovered, is to jump before my brain and body notice what I'm doing. And then, to do it again right away, to prove that the first plunge wasn't a fluke. So that the next time I'm at the pool, it feels like nothing. So that the fear moves into the realm of distant memory, like the day/night/

day when I gave birth to my daughter or the dinner in my teens when my parents announced they were separating.

Terrifying, life-altering, but not relevant to the present moment.

Which is how I knew it was time to try the five-metre board. Next time, maybe, I'll jump head first.

| It's 10:30 PM on Thursday. After picking up the girl from daycare, making dinner, and putting on a load of laundry, I'm done. I have no energy left for anything that requires careful attention. So even though I was hoping to get some writing done, tonight is NOT the night.

Michael is already on the couch, having just started a program he'd PVRed. I sit down next to him, but I'm feeling restless.

I look at the basket of clean laundry on the floor, waiting to be folded, to be hauled upstairs and put away. I look at my laptop, sitting on the coffee table, waiting for me to write the next thing, to empty myself out. I sigh.

Mike hits the pause button on the remote. And gives me a significant look.

"I think I might go for a walk," I say. I'd ask him to join me—I could use some hand-holding and companionable silence—but someone has to stay home with the girl.

"Okay," he says. "The last time I went, I walked up Wolseley and then back on Portage. It was a good route."

"Yeah," I say, but I already know I won't go that way: too many buses and cars, brake lights and exhaust. It's the opposite of what I want, which is the treed expanse of the Wolseley–Wellington loop.

The treed expanse...and the darkness.

"Have a good walk!" Mike calls out, as I close the door behind me. "Be careful!"

| I try to walk the loop at least a couple of times a week.

The Wolseley half is a straight shot through my treed middle-class neighbourhood, adjacent to Winnipeg's downtown. It's notorious for being a left-wing enclave and is nicknamed The Granola Belt. Lots of mature/dying elms, lots of shrubs and boulevard gardens.

The Wellington half runs on a parallel course through the richer neighbourhood on the other side of the river. More trees, mature oaks and elms and conifers, but also long swathes of grass, maintained by landscaping companies. When my daughter was small, she dubbed it "Mansion Street." Between· the two neighbourhoods, the dirty hippies and the robber barons, there's a park and a train bridge with a pedestrian lane that crosses the river.

As I walk up Wolseley Avenue, passing my daughter's school on the left, and then Aubrey Playground, and then Wolseley School on my right, everything is familiar: middle-aged dog walkers, hipsters on bikes, joggers in neon athletic gear.

At the entrance to the park, I still have a choice: turning right would take me up to Portage Avenue, one of Winnipeg's main drags. It's well-lit, with convenience stores and gas stations and places that sell pizza by the slice.

Turning left will take me into the park, where there are few lights and no houses, only a long expanse of riverbank and train tracks and porous dark.

I turn left.

| In my twenties, I walked everywhere. Late at night, in "bad" neighbourhoods, by myself. I was a careful walker, acutely aware of who was sharing the sidewalk with me, how close they were, and whether or not they looked dangerous. I never put myself in bad situations, which meant no back alleys or

dead ends. And if someone looked dubious, I nonchalantly crossed the street.

What's more, I walked with confidence and made a point of looking everyone in the eye.

I'm here, my body language said. *I see you.*

I know I had the advantage of being white and middle class. Which conferred a variety of advantages, not the least of which was knowing that if someone tried anything, if I were attacked, people—shop owners, taxi drivers, bystanders, the authorities—would probably help me.

I was also six feet tall, six-foot-two in the army boots I affected in those days, and substantially built. So I knew I wasn't anyone's preferred prey: smaller, slighter women or men were easier pickings.

Sometimes, when my hair was tied back, other women would mistake my silhouette for a man's and move to avoid me. They'd cross the street or peer at me with scared eyes as we passed on the sidewalk.

I tried to reassure them, sometimes by pulling out and playing with my pony tail—*See my long hair? I'm a girl like you, I'm not going to hurt you.*—sometimes by just saying hello. Because the last thing I wanted was to ramp up someone else's fear.

My insistence on walking alone at night used to make people mad. They'd insist, more and more aggressively, on driving me home: What do you mean, you *want* to walk home? Do you *want* to get raped?

My answer was always that I was careful, that nothing had ever happened. That it had been years of me walking. They gave me significant looks and left me to my dubious choices.

| As I approach the small hill in the middle of the park, I remember a walk here two years ago with my friend Tessa.

It was twilight and we'd been chatting as we climbed the hill, focused on each other instead of what was ahead of us.

We stopped short when we saw two men crouched over a woman on the ground, a bike with a spinning wheel nearby.

And it was absolutely the last thing I wanted to see: an Indigenous woman lying still on the ground, two white men crouched over her...

And then, the men—teenaged boys—turned to look at us with big scared eyes. They'd come upon her, already on the ground, and they'd wanted to help. But they didn't know what to do. We told them we'd take care of her and then called—and waited for—an ambulance. The teenagers ran away oh-so-gratefully.

Tessa went out to meet the ambulance. I waited with the woman, who woke, confused, and confided that she was pregnant before having a seizure and passing out again. Tessa and I were both glad, separately and together, when flashing lights signaled that paramedics had arrived.

As I crest the hill, I make a fleeting wish that the woman is safe now but also reach into my bag and grab my cell phone. I hit the flashlight icon with my thumb and pick up the pace.

So I don't get caught in the darkest part of the park or in the middle of the train bridge, so I won't be raped and left for dead. I am afraid, breathing quickly, my stomach clenched, my brain nattering.

Is that someone ahead? Shit! It is! I bet this is where that knife fight I read about in the paper happened. Okay, he's walking towards me...

| Looking back, I realize that I was not very afraid in my thirties: I was too busy writing and working and parenting my daughter. I was anxious I would maybe never publish more than a few poems, even though I'd been writing since I was

thirteen. But then my first book came out. I was worried that I wouldn't be a good parent to my daughter, that she couldn't possibly flourish under my care. But my daughter was resolutely healthy and even easy to care for.

What's more, I had an emotional stability, an easiness about my place in the world, that I now envy.

My forties have been dominated by my friends' divorces, my father's slide into dementia, and my aging woman's body.

I am surprised to be struggling with perimenopause, with heavy bleeding and anemia and light-headedness, with weight gain and white hairs jutting out at my hairline. For the first time in years, I have bled through my pants. I have bled any number of times on my office chair.

Everyone—my peers, my parents, myself—seems to be fragile in ways that I hadn't noticed before.

And I don't know what to do with that. If I'm being honest, the best part about flinging myself off the diving boards is the admiring glances of the boneless preteens, who shoot themselves off the diving boards like they're both the cannon and the cannonball.

While they might not be afraid, they understand that other people could be. Also, most of the time, their parents are not on the boards beside them.

My daughter's reaction to the diving boards, sometimes, is to weep with fear and frustration, standing two feet back from the edge. She refuses to jump but refuses to back down, either.

Fresh from my own plunge, I stand next to her, full of exasperated admiration. I know she's neck-deep in irrational, choking fear, but I still try to persuade her to jump. Part of my project as a parent is to take her on adventures: to get her to climb things, to get dirty, to take risks. So we do the diving boards together.

But my daughter isn't unique in her fear. Every time we go swimming, there are one or two little girls on the highest board, caught in the same feedback loop. The longer they stand there, the louder the chorus of people cheering them on gets: siblings and strangers, people who wouldn't speak to each other otherwise. The encouragement isn't what makes the little girls finally jump, of course. They get embarrassed about being scared or the lifeguard announces that the pool is about to close. But there's nothing like watching them emerge from the water, hearing the hubbub, having somehow turned themselves into wet heroes...

I wonder, does doing the Wolseley–Wellington loop at night make me a hero? Does it make me brave?

| When I was at university, the Womyn's Centre would organize annual Take Back the Night marches. The idea was that a group of women could walk, together, without fear. There were also organized Safe Walk patrols on campus, where volunteers would walk women to their nearby houses or cars. And while I sympathized, I never joined the Take Back the Night marches and I never used Safe Walk: it didn't feel like I needed them, like they were meant for me.

Twenty years later, there are still women being attacked in back alleys and parks and on their way home from work. They're literally being raped and thrown in the river. They're being attacked and attacked, generations of girls, before and after me.

And it's so much worse if you're not white or middle class, for queer or trans people, for Indigenous women, who wear their fear in the form of Missing and Murdered Indigenous Women wristbands inscribed with "Am I next?"

"Am I next?" is the most terrifying question I can think of.

A notice for this year's march floated through my Facebook newsfeed this week. I still won't be going, but this time, I can acknowledge that women walking alone at night were vulnerable then and they're vulnerable now, whether or not I choose to participate.

| Up close, I see that the man approaching me is just another someone on a walk. I feel foolish.

I feel brave.

I've crossed the bridge and am halfway down Wellington Crescent when I suddenly come upon a fawn, with a summer's growth on her, standing in a pool of light in the middle of the broad and leafy boulevard.

Even though deer sightings are common in the city, even though deer are considered pests by most people, there *is* a magic here: something alive in the night with me. Something utterly non-threatening.

Because there is no way to be afraid of a fawn.

And she is still in a dim pool of light from a streetlamp and it takes me a second to realize that she's staring back at me. That she's assessing, over and over and over, whether or not I pose a threat, whether or not she should be afraid of me.

I am fifteen feet away, stopped.

And I could stand in the darkness and watch her watch me forever.

And then a jogger runs down the gravel path towards us and the fawn lopes off to the other side of the road and the deeper darkness there. But not before being narrowly missed by a car. And then there is a doe, probably her mother, who runs after the fawn, more confidently crossing both lanes of traffic.

After that, I keep on seeing deer in the outlines of park benches and tree limbs even though I know every bench along this route and this is the first time I've spotted deer.

| If you were to ask me why I walk the Wolseley–Wellington loop at night, I'd probably say it's for the stillness of the trees, the novel emptiness of what is normally a well-used path. That the trees look different at night and I have an idea that I am different, walking underneath them.

My second, less-fanciful answer would be that I need exercise and that it's easier for me to go walking after the girl has gone to bed. That the loop, specifically, is the perfect distance for a walk, its six kilometres taking me just over an hour.

If I were really feeling expansive, I'd say that I rely on the mechanics of walking itself, its effects on my body and brain—my digestive system kick-started, my mood improved—to take away some of my aches. That I know I'll be thinking better by walk's end.

What's more, studies have shown that exercise has multiple beneficial effects and that walking in a wooded or even a semi-wooded space has additional benefits over, say, walking on a treadmill or around a track.

All these reasons are valid. But the real answer, the thing that drives me out the door, is neither practical nor pretty: Walking the loop at night, by myself, throwing my eyes up into the branches of the nighttime trees like they were a pair of fleeing birds, replaces my stupid ennui with the specific animal fear of someone lunging towards me out of the dark.

It kicks my brain into a different gear. Which is usually enough.

| I am nearly at the Maryland Street Bridge and the entrance to my own neighbourhood, the emptied-out preserve that is Wellington Crescent at night behind me, when someone runs by me. He is big and fast.

I startle *hard*, hand on my heart, and he doesn't even notice, cocooned in his workout gear, wired into his playlist.

I'm scared.

But suddenly, I realize how absurd this is, and I want nothing more than to throw down the bundle of fear I've willfully—deliberately—carried for the past forty-five minutes. My brain starts nattering at me: What am I doing? I *never* would have walked here in my twenties! Never!

The cardinal rule of my twenties was that if I was walking at night, I looked for bright busy streets. Where I could see people coming for miles. Where there were stores and restaurants to slip into if I needed to.

This is the opposite of that.

Stands of trees are just as beautiful at night as they are during the day. But at night, they create pools of shade, provide cover for both real and imaginary bad guys.

So what am I doing, tugging my leaky body along like a broken kite? Working with fear? No. I'm just scaring myself, as a way of managing my anxiety over getting older, over whether or not I matter.

I'm not being brave by walking this route at night: I'm being foolhardy.

I still believe in working with fear, with uncertainty. My stints at the edge of the diving board are just the most obvious, but I work with uncertainty all the time: I take myself on adventures and not just the ones that are safe for my daughter. In my writing, I try to work at the very edge of what's possible for me. That's scary. Sometimes—often—that means failing.

I believe that if I don't walk the edge of fear and uncertainty, I'll never move forward.

But these nighttime walks of the Wolseley–Wellington loop are not a good way of working with fear: there's no overcoming it, no way of putting this fear behind me, of learning from it.

Because as long as people hurt other people, as long people are seen as targets, the fear of walking alone, at night, in vulnerable locations, is actually a reasonable one. Should the streets be safe? Yes. Are they safe most of the time? Yes, but people are still sometimes mugged, still raped.

Because there's no outrunning this body.

There's also my daughter to think of. When she's in her twenties, I want her to be stubborn and independent in her own way, to march towards the edges of what she's capable of. To leap. When she's in her forties, I want her to be brave and obstinate in her own way, to learn and relearn all the paths that will bring her meaning and purpose.

But the last thing I want is for her to take unnecessary risks.

And here I am, modeling risky behaviour...

Which means that I have to stop doing this, right now, because walking the Wolseley–Wellington loop at night by myself is nothing—nothing—but a beautiful/dead end.

Who Counts the Years?

MAUREEN BUSH

"HOW OLD ARE YOU?" an eight-year-old boy asked in a school session. Three classes of Grade 3 kids crowded the classroom floor, their teachers on chairs nearby. I'd talked about my books and we'd made up a wild story, then moved on to questions. A sea of hands waved, everyone eager. This question of the author's age was of perennial interest to children. Teachers cringed, and often scolded. "You don't ask that!"

But I always answered. It's important for kids to know that a meaningful life doesn't end at twenty-nine, that people can do interesting things all through their lives.

"How old were you when you started writing books for kids?"

"About forty."

"How old are you now?"

"Fifty-five."

Eyes widened. "Wow! You don't look fifty-five."

I shrugged. "This is what fifty-five looks like."

I heard a rustle around the room, like when little kids get bored and start playing with the Velcro on their shoes. Except this was the adults. I felt the thought rippling through: *This is not what fifty-five looks like!*

I thought but didn't say, *I meditate.*

| When I learned to meditate, I learned to relax. I'd sit, concentrating on a flame or a photo or my breath, and perhaps for a few moments, my endless thoughts would pause. As I sank into that moment, the muscles in my face relaxed and the tension in my gut eased, until I remembered, and thoughts and tensions flooded back.

Over and over, every day, I sat in silence, in stillness. I'd recite a mantra, or focus on my breath, learning to slow my mind, to not be caught up in the endless rush of thinking thinking thinking. I started to notice a gap between thoughts, a break in the endless stream. I'd rest in the pause between breaths, *inhale–exhale–pause*, and let my thoughts pause, too, silent for that brief moment. Slowly, painfully slowly, my mind became quieter.

My first retreat, a weekend in Whistler, was profoundly quiet, a deep drop into meditation. When I flew home, people in the Vancouver airport looked wound up, tense and angry. I couldn't figure out what was wrong until I realized I'd spent the weekend with people whose faces had softened into deep relaxation.

I kept meditating, fifteen years of learning not to wind up into daily inevitable stresses, slowly letting go of deeper tensions. They lived in my body, in my back and gut and face. Slowly, so slowly I didn't notice, they left, taking with them the knotted muscles, the clenched fists, the tight jaw. Let go of the trauma, and the body changes.

| It's hard to guess the age of long-term meditators. I discovered that a friend I thought my age is ten years older. There's

an ageless quality to older Buddhists, as if they inhabit a liminal space of timelessness. Indeed, they do.

Deep spiritual work, which sounds wild and is even wilder to experience, moves meditators into timelessness. Spacelessness. Formlessness. As a meditator, I learn to exist in the present moment in my daily life, and occasionally slip into timelessness.

Of course, meditators die, like everyone else. The human form is finite. But the fear of death leaves. I know people who've lost that fear through a near-death experience, or a spiritual awakening. Once I had seen the oneness of everything, there was no reason to fear death. Dying can be excruciatingly painful and losing a loved one is a deep loss. But personal death? That feels like a doorway, a step into something new, the next great adventure, and when my body becomes frail, a welcome one. Death is a dance of energy, not a tragedy. And living without a fear of death? That's another tension gone.

| As I drop emotional baggage and open to the oneness of the universe, everything becomes beautiful. The oldest, most deeply wrinkled face? Like the bark of a beloved tree. A bent, crippled body? My hands reach out in love, longing to heal.

Meditators let go of society's assumptions and pressures, beliefs and values about aging. Instead we rest in silence, in vastness. Our faces light up, eyes dancing, warmth beaming out. And no one counts the years.

Intent to Forgive

JOY KOGAWA

Excerpt from a work in progress

IN HER EIGHTIES, my mother suffered from severe deafness and dementia. My brother and I are in our mid-eighties now. I share my mother's deafness, my brother her dementia, though I, too, recognize the signs of cognitive decline.

I call my brother almost daily. He doesn't know who I am. He will say things like, "You're Joy? That's my sister's name."

"Yes. I'm your sister."

"Oh, I haven't heard from you in a long time. Where do you live?"

"In Toronto."

"You're in Tronna? I'm in Seattle. It's 6:00 o'clock here. It must be 9:00 where you are."

"Yes. That's right. I'm three hours away. It's nine at night."

"It's six in the morning here."

He can still spell. We sing hymns. He remembers living in Vancouver and Slocan, BC, and later, after the war, in Coaldale in southern Alberta. We were teenagers there in the early '50s. My brother was the darling of his teachers and his parents.

Last year a friend, Shirley, and I took an online test for dementia from Baycrest. We both scored abysmally low. I couldn't put names to faces, except Asian faces. It impels me to attempt to write *Intent to Forgive* while I still can, if I still can.

Forgiveness is the task I feel for this final leg of the journey. For me, it's eternity's path.

There is in my diary a growing list of notions arising from dreams, conversations, mostly out of nowhere, mostly first thing in the morning. I picture them as small rafts bobbing along on the sea. They come in handy during midnight storms when I'm floundering—little safety rafts of comforting, useful notions to hang on to.

Here are a few:

If you announce love, love will arrive.
Time expands for the work of love.
Time shrinks for the work of money.
Or, if you run after money, freedom runs from you.
To be fully known is to be fully loved.
The food of friendship is light. Light is two parts love,
    one part truth.
Freedom is to trust always.
The least visible is the most powerful.
The best friend is hiding in the enemy.
Mercy and abundance are one.
As the petals fade, the seed grows; as flesh weakens,
    the spirit wakens.

Notions are seeds. They lie dormant until they are planted and watered in a person's life. I think of the willingness to forgive and the desire to forgive as helpful for peace.

Forgiveness eases the heart of the forgiver. But it's hard. Maybe it's one of the hardest of struggles. Impossible even.

Many tasks of forgiveness are lined up ahead, signposts on the road. One that is consuming me is the need to forgive myself for not protecting a friend. I did try. But failed. I also want to be able to forgive the people who I see as having harmed my friend. But I'm failing at that too. Nevertheless, I need to try. Failure is fine. In fact, it's more than fine. Failure is proof I tried.

"Failure is fine," is a useful adage for old age with its growing vulnerability and other chills of a wintry season. We, mere mortals, cannot do what we cannot do. We've heard it said that "to err is human; to forgive, divine."

What I'm finding is that the intention to forgive is more than good enough. As I continue to intend, as my hand reaches out and touches the handle of the door but does not have the wherewithal to turn it, a startling thing happens. The forgiveness door opens from the other side. And gifts— amazing, surprising gifts—come pummelling through that crack. The "us and them" world dissolves for a moment and the intent to forgive is replaced by a thankful heart.

Every speck of thankfulness helps the world. This may be just another notion, but I hold to it. It's a fine way to be useful, even if you're just lying in a hospital bed wondering what the point of it all is.

Meister Eckhart said, "If the only prayer you said in your whole life was 'Thank you,' that would suffice."

A barn swallow relative to objects and places

WENDY MCGRATH

you are the weight of one house key
two pencils
20 paperclips

you build your nest in
barn
bridge
culvert

because you want humans
to hear you above so much pointless noise
an open mouth is your default position
to sing to eat or yawn
I turn my house key in the lock and open my mouth to shout
    to an empty house
where I keep two pencils in a hand-blown glass cup made
    by my son
with 20 paperclips that have magnetized all on their own
but I swallow this emptiness and simply shape my hands
    into a nest

the petals in me

LAURIE MACFAYDEN

i am the one who paints the trees
the heart of a maiden but never a bride
soon to be called crone
if i am called at all

i am achy limbs and dodgy memory
high salt in the blood and dimming vision
i am mostly iris, hint of daffodil
the reach of ambitious sunflower, bending
turning from shade whenever possible
never as quick or nimble
as the petals in me used to be
as i once was
as i remember

forever wordsmith, painter; forever wishing i were pilot
i am one who walks (more slowly) and swims (hardly ever)
i still stare at the wild blue, ponder clouds
in awe, feeling small and pointless
forever buoyed by soft air and melody

i am an old woman
content now to think more and talk less
of course i want justice, and peace,
and to live inside the authentic
under a wide-brimmed hat

i cast out the shaming mirror.
i don't care how i look.
i want to be kind. i want to be good.

ELDERS

Listen

ANNE SORBIE

I

Your bloody daughter has done it again. First it was your
wife's license. And maybe that was warranted. Your wife did
tell you about that time she was three-quarters of the way
through a stop sign before she realized. And about that other
time when she said she almost ran down a man on a bike. So
taking away your wife's license was probably warranted. But.
This time your offspring wants yours. And it's undeserved.

Your bloody daughter got involved in your life while you
were at the stroke rehabilitation centre for those two or three
months. And she showed up there every single day. There they
had the nerve to use an occupational therapist to *teach you*
how to swallow. As if that was something you'd never done
before. And she was in on it: *encouraging you* to look in a mirror
while you ate. Bloody hell. It was there, too, that they forced
you to go to session after session with a physiotherapist and a
speech therapist. You didn't care if you had a wee limp on the
right side, or about the droop and the slur. You would've
dealt with all that. You could've even had preferred parking.

But. There was nothing preferential mentioned when you
heard your bloody daughter and the bitch cardiologist talking

about your driver's license. Excuse me. The female doctor. The one who acted as if she had every right to tell you what to do. The same one who told your son to calm down that one morning. Or she'd have him removed. Possibly even banned. All he did was to put her in her place. To stick up for you. Who the hell did she, did they think they were anyway?

Today your bloody daughter is driving you to that place where you have to prove you are worthy of a driver's license. She took your wife there, too. To make it all official and governmental. But this time she's messing with the wrong man. You signed the forms all right. And they can review them until they're blue in the face. You'll show them. You are still equipped.

You're in your bloody daughter's car. Her Auto Union Deutsche car. She's so stupid she probably doesn't even know that while the car name has a German root, Audi is the Latin for "listen." But that's ironic, because as you've told your son over and over again, she never listens. Just as an example, she didn't hear you when you said she was to bring you the keys to your vehicle. So you showed her.

You took a taxi to the house. Not her house. Your own house, when you had a day pass. You got the emergency key from the magnetic box inside the front bumper and you took the van out to Tim Hortons. It wasn't far. And you were lucky. It was the neighbourhood constable who's been around for donkey's years that reprimanded you when you accidentally ripped off your right-side mirror on the chain-link fence near the drive-through. Lucky because he let you buy your ham and cheese before he and his partner drove you and your van back to the house where he made you surrender the key. Where he called you another taxi that took you back to the stroke rehabilitation place. Lucky, too, because he parked the van at the side of the garage right where your bloody daughter had put it three months before.

The other day, you thought you'd try something else. You got one of the volunteer girlies to look up Car2Go for you online. You thought you were really going to be able to register. That you'd really and truly be good to go. And that your bloody daughter and the bitch doctor would never know. You even remembered your credit card number. But when the thingy asked for your driver's license details it was game over. Until then you imagined hopping into one of those wee Daimlers whenever you wanted, daughters and doctors be damned. Instead, some outfit called Driving Miss Daisy is phoning you to *plan your outings*. To Tai Chi, the bank and the barber, even the bottle depot.

This afternoon, before you start, you know that you're going to fail the test to prove you can drive. It involves a computer and typing. You've never had to type anything. That's something your wife was happy to do and that you were happy to let her do. Even all that online banking stuff. It wasn't like she could sit at the makeshift desk in the dining room and steal your money without you knowing.

After the test you tell your bloody daughter how stupid the exam was. And. You want to know why the idiot man didn't let you do the road test. You tell your bloody daughter there must be some kind of effing mistake. And mark. You never use that word unless it's really warranted. You've repaired and driven all manner of vehicles and vessels in your life. From the 1941 Bentley sedan that you bought and fixed up, to the ships' sonars you worked on in Aberdeen, to your first Canadian car, a red and white International Harvester Travelall, to the tanks and armoured vehicles you nursed to life on CFB Calgary.

You tell your bloody daughter that mistakes abound. You talk about the female cardiologist. You yell about the test results that prevented you from moving back into your own home. You're screaming and yelling at her when she drives up to the front of your *new* assisted living place. You get out, and while gripping the handle of the passenger door, you bend over slightly, make sure she can see your face. You tell her you are hiring a taxi as soon as she's gone. That you're going to Nissan to test-drive a Cube and that she can't stop you.

When she says, and very gently, I'm so sorry Dad. And follows that even more quietly with, You can't do that without a license. You let your bloody daughter have it.

You say the thing you've never told her, her whole life. The thing that always embarrassed your wife. The thing that always kept your wedding anniversary a low-key event, no matter the number of years. There are only six and a half months between your wedding day and your eldest daughter's birthday. You! You bellow in front of all the old people getting off the lodge bus and walking past you to the front door. YOU, you repeat, even though everything inside your head tells you not to. YOU! You yell at the top of your battered old lungs: YOU were a misssss-take!

The happy murmurings of the people going inside are suddenly absent. You don't even hear the slamming of the car door and you give it everything you've got. The air around you is silent. You watch the silver Deutsch Auto Union car drive away. You are triumphant.

One day later on, it seems like a decade since you lost your driver's license. But the staff assures you that you've been living in the lodge for just a year. It's then you wonder if it's really been that long since you've had a visit from your bloody daughter.

II

I am not bloody although I am a daughter. I am the family feminist. An ideal. I'm also the family fixer. When you need to solve something or to get something? I am the person you come to. You mention A and I can tell you how to get to B. Got a problem with XYZ? Don't worry. I can show you how easy it is to get back to ABC. That doesn't mean you have to involve me in the details as you go. Just report back when you achieve the thing and we can celebrate your success together! That's right. The minutiae are not, usually, my responsibility.

Exception? The parent trap. That's right. I really said that. Excuse me, caregiver role. Your parents begin to age out and all that lovely close and not, distance you had from them as your children became adults and you began to enjoy real freedom? That all begins to unravel and you are back being a (m)other again. Still someone's daughter. Still a feminist, and usually. Wait. No. Never. Quite ideal.

Every minute of every day is tangled in a web of health care and appointments. Making them. Keeping them. Driving to and fro. The preparing to drive to and fro. The feeding and the toileting. Before. During. After. The carrying of another bag with extra underwear or even diapers, wipes, latex gloves, socks, a pair of dry shoes. And. There are other times when you wish you'd included a mask or a pair of clear wrap-around glasses in that bag. But. You do keep a little bottle of lavender oil in the small zipper section where you put your car keys so you don't lose track of them in the midst of the mayhem. And then. You discover there's something else. Foot care. Nails curving over the top of the toes. No wonder your spry mother didn't want to go for her usual long walks.

The chaos is at its worst when the aged parent has to be moved. Out of home and into housing. The pickings are slim. Even when you find a way to pay a premium. The established places aren't so fresh, and in the newly opened, the well-meaning staffers don't have answers to questions like: Why is the "hospital-like bed" barely wide enough for one person? Or why are the shower or the toilet or the alarm monitoring system not working?

And then an even funnier thing happens. After I weather the storms and the surgeries and the meds, the mother (now dead) and father who has retreated back to his childhood. I have a double-digit birthday that begins and ends with fives. And. *My* youngest adult daughter declares, *you are a golden girl*. And my child promises to ship me *off to Shady Pines*, she says, joking. If *I* don't behave. And unexpectedly *I am* there. At the top of a hill from where I can clearly see: the slippery slope.

I stand and I look and at the top is the aging in place, place. And from there I experience my very own introduction to the idea of the suddenly out of control. To the slap of the calendar. To the slip of the tongue that spouts all the words I taught it to say. I wanted another generation of fit fabulous fully formed feminists. And. Lucky me. I have two. They know how to speak. How to voice. How to say. Dare I say it? They are just like me! I decide I have to be nicer to them.

My daughters assure me they will do it all for me. Because to be sure, in the next while there'll be an app for elder care. The same way there is one now for the caring for humans at the beginning of life. It's called The Wonder Weeks. Takes all the guesswork out of what's going on in. Say. Week 13 when the baby goes through a leap and the parents can expect a surge in eating on demand. The grandmother and her experiences are hardly ever called upon. Maybe for something absolutely necessary. Such as a few hours of sleep.

And so. I think they should invent an Elder app. Then. Most care issues can be predicted or looked up instantly.

Users can go directly to Amazon. For the shower bars and the raised toilet seats, the discreet bulgy panties, the support socks. I'm sure that they'll ensure those arrive at my door. In a timely fashion. In a brown box. No one will know what's inside. Except for the occasional porch bandit. And he or she will surely be surprised after unpacking a bubble-wrapped, hand-held urinal.

And me? I'll be an orphan. But I'll still be a feminist. Although by then, I may finally be ideal. My voice might grow quiet. And. My vectors may be lost in the ventriloquism of my type A to B, XY super Z, she/her daughters.

And then *I'll* be told not to worry, just to relax. I'm praying that the location of relaxing is going to be in the wheelhouse of my Vancouver daughter. In the steam of the Norwegian sauna in the brightly lit walkout basement of the net-zero elder complex in which I am installed. The one with the high-tech robo living room. In a building so well manufactured I won't care if I see out the real windows to the ocean or the valley and the mountains.

And one day all I'll have to do is take a sip. And not one tiny speck of fear will dot my aura. Not a whit of worry will appear. Thanks to the ultimate drink. Which will surely be available by then. And by the way, girls, I'd like to take mine with a little champagne. Organic. French. Don't forget to do my hair and my nails. And please, please pay attention to my feet. They are already quite sensitive.

And then I will drift off. I promise. Soft. And lickety-split. I'll fade from my body. And all I will ask, all I've ever asked, is that you hold to your own ideals. At least until that day arrives. The one on which one of your children, or perhaps maybe a dear and close friend, will let you know you where you stand. And surprisingly and unexpectedly *you* will be there! That's right. At the top of the proverbial hill.

Back to the Garden

ELIZABETH HAYNES

THE GROUNDS of the Mayan Palace complex are lush
and expansive; the ocean just strolling distance away. The
sun flames out in spectacular fashion. There is yoga in the
Ramada, beach volleyball, ping pong, and golf. Happy hour
starts early and slides into happy half day. "The compound,"
as my dad calls it, is isolated at the end of a long road. Puerto
Vallarta, with its art galleries and museums, is a half-hour taxi
ride away. My octogenarian parents, Jessie and Sterling, are
Prairie people. They don't golf. They don't swim much. They
haven't been to the ocean in years.

I am here because they wanted to escape winter. Traded in
their rural timeshare for this fancy one. When I arrived, Dad
told me Mom got lost in the huge dining room one breakfast. She's always been directionally challenged, perhaps as
a result of her Saskatchewan childhood, where everything is
always in plain sight.

Mom is eager to show me the flora and fauna. We stroll
the grounds at dusk, stopping beside a tea-coloured pond.
Cormorants and herons hide in the shadows. The tangerine
sun slides into the water. She points to a shore bird, his long
beak bobbing as he siphons up dinner.

"Do you remember the name of that one, dear?"

"I think you're confusing me with another daughter," I joke. Though my three sisters and I were given detailed information about the plumage and habits of the cedar waxwings, juncos, and yellow-bellied sapsuckers that perched on the feeder outside our dining-room window in Kamloops, I was terrible at remembering their names. According to my mother, even starlings are darlings. She has never met a bird she doesn't like.

On the way back to our suite, she recites the names of flowers and bushes, still hoping to educate her eldest: fish-bone cactus, Mexican marigold. Mom has never met a flower she doesn't like either, even weedy volunteers that spread through prairie like fire through fescue. Sadly, I am also bad on flowers.

Growing up in Biggar, Saskatchewan, in the 1930s, my mom, Jessie, learned to garden from her Scottish mother, my grandmother Jean. Grandma grew radishes, lettuce, and peas. Green and yellow beans. Turnips, parsnips, carrots, watercress, and potatoes. Apple trees and currant bushes: black, red, white Missouri. When I was a child, from the muddy days of early spring through leaf-crunching fall, my mom could be found outside, on her knees, an ice-cream bucket with her trowel, shears, and spade by her side. She planted her rock garden, pruned the rhodos, weeded the carrots, and prepared her gardens for winter. Mom planted purple-red Italian tomatoes that flourished in the long, sunny summers. She grew peas, beans, carrots. Giant zucchini kept us supplied with green bread. She gave us our own section of the garden to weed and water, so we'd grow green thumbs, too.

| Mom and I are heading to the Puerto Vallarta botanical gardens outside of town. Walking is difficult for Dad so he's

decided to stay at the "compound." Mom is excited to see the gardens, despite an unpredictable ankle that makes walking on uneven surfaces tricky. We take a cab and alight in the centre of town. I walk behind my small mother to the bus stop to make sure she doesn't get distracted by some natural wonder and stumble. When we were kids, all my sisters and I had to do to distract her from, say, the fact that we had housework or dishes to do, was ask her to identify a bird. Or to help us find mariposa lilies and yellow Johnny jump-ups in the sage-covered hills behind our rambling old house.

The bus to the gardens winds past emerald cliffs, clattering around bends to reveal glimpses of the ocean below. How beautiful this place must have been when it was just a small fishing village, before tourists and timeshares. We get off at the top of a hill, cross the highway, and walk down to the gardens, where we lunch. The resident macaw perches on the railing beside us, waiting for his close-up perhaps. We view the orchid collection, admire one like our childhood favourite, lady's slipper, then hike the path that meanders past other lovelies: bromeliads, sedum, agave. The footing is tricky, but Mom wants to walk all the trails and insists on descending right to the stream. We pick our way along until blocked by boulders.

"It's getting rough, Mom, and these rocks look slippery and hard to get around. I think we should turn back."

"Oh, let's just go a little farther."

"I don't want you to fall, Mom. If you hurt yourself, Dad will kill me."

"Come on," she urges. She grabs my hand, like I'm her best childhood friend, Didi, and they're searching the coulees for crocuses. "Let's just see what's around that next bend."

As a child, Mom had the freedom to explore wherever she wanted: in the town, the surrounding coulees, the railyard where her Scottish dad worked as a hostler's helper, her uncle's farm. A freedom she extended to her daughters, handing us lunches and a Thermos full of water as she sent us up into the hills to explore. She kept dead birds she had found in baggies in the freezer, to later give to her friend, Anna, a fellow naturalist and amateur taxidermist. Mom grew herbs in little cups in our cluttered kitchen beside glasses with toothpick-impaled avocado pits in water and the drying wishbones of various holiday birds awaiting our wishes.

When she was little and there were chores to do, my mother ran away. When my grandma tried to show her how to can preserves or make a pie crust, she'd slip out the back door. I imagine Mom and Didi, armed with syrup pails for Saskatoon berries, roaming far and wide, missing dinner.

I picture them on their backs in my great-uncle's wheat field, counting cloud animals and red-tailed hawks in that big sky.

| On our second last day at the compound, we take a tour with my parents' favourite socialist tour guide, Miguel, who had previously escorted them on a tour of a mining town and coffee plantation. A tour which, to their delight, included a detailed labour history. Our destination: a distant Huichol village. It will be a long bus ride, I warn them, six hours on bad roads, I say, but fascinated by the Huichol yarn and bead art they've seen in town, they are determined to go. We eventually find ourselves in a tiny cluster of huts on the top of a hill, overlooking a wide valley. Miguel has only recently started bringing tourists here and cautions us to be respectful and polite. Yes, the villagers may be poor, but they are strong people with an ancient spiritual tradition that includes honouring the peyote. This sacred plant is featured in their art, yarn paintings, and bead-encrusted gourds. Which we

should buy, Miguel says. One or more pieces per family, he suggests. As Dad chats with the teenaged sellers in Spanglish, selecting paintings for my sisters, Mom and I wander to the edge of a cliff. She pulls out her binoculars and we watch the raptors riding up and down the sky.

| My mother once told me this story. It was 1953. She had left Carrot River, where she was adjudicating a drama festival, in a blizzard on a train bound for Nipawin, where she was living and teaching. The track hadn't been cleared of snow and the train couldn't continue. The conductor told my mother and the four other people on board to get off and walk to the railway tracks that intersected their line and had been cleared. One of the five was a pregnant woman. The wind whirled snow around them. Visibility dropped. The little group walked through knee-high drifts as the snow got heavier and the temperature fell. Finally, someone thought he saw a distant farmhouse, and they left the safety of the tracks, wading through waist-deep snow toward that farm-house, which I imagine kept disappearing and reappearing, house then mirage, house, mirage. House. The farmer and his wife welcomed the exhausted band, let them warm up, fed them, and drove them to the railway station.

I suspect that they could have easily been lost in that bliz-zard, could have succumbed to the cold, died of hypothermia. But my mother related this story with a smile on her face. They were almost lost, yes. It was cold. It was difficult. But she met some wonderful people—her fellow travellers, the farmhouse couple who were so kind and generous. And wasn't it all such a great adventure?

| In retirement, my mother took up kadō, the Japanese way of the flowers. The drained and covered hot tub in their

Kelowna home, initially installed to ease arthritic joints, became the "ikebana table." Mom collected interesting-looking twigs and branches. Cut bits of Oregon grape and brought in a single iris, tulip, sunflower from her garden. She started an ikebana club, hired a local teacher, studied with a sensei who came from Japan to teach classes. Spent hours collecting and arranging. Gave up the practice only when her arthritic fingers refused to co-operate any more, to snip and bend, to fashion the scalene triangle symbolizing heaven, human, earth. She gave up quietly. Without a fuss. She still had her garden.

I've always preferred living in sky-full places. As a young woman, I spent two winters in Terrace, BC, where the fog and winter inversions, the looming mountains, withered my spirit, became heavy. A burden.

My mother Jessie's maiden name is Porter, which means a carrier of burdens. But I think my mother, and her mother before her, carried their burdens lightly. My grandma Jean's loss of her first husband and three brothers in World War I and the Spanish flu epidemic; Grandma's only living sibling, her beloved sister, Jessie, too far away to visit in Scotland. My Jessie's illnesses and battles.

My Jessie taught me to look at what was below me: to search a coulee bank for the first spring flowers, to spy the red of spawning salmon in the sun-dappled creeks in the fall. To look up for the red-winged blackbird flitting along the bulrushes; the hawk riding air.

Ten years after that Mexico trip, my parents live in a seniors' "resort" in Kelowna. Chosen for its location beside a nature trail and creek and because there are raised plots where they can plant a small garden. My Jessie can enjoy nature, pushing her walker down the path, her chest still tender from recent surgery—searching for the great horned owl she has once seen; the golden eyes she hopes to see; the first yellow balsam roots of spring.

Upriver

ROBERTA REES

WHERE TO START, this issue of looking. Of looking good. Of age.

Always circling back to my mother. "We're born to die, it's what we do in between that counts."

To her death. Her youth.

My youth. My inevitable death.

Circling until we can't.

Look.

"You look just like Shirley Temple," the man said when he stepped out from the shadows of the warehouse two doors down from her house, her mother in bed struggling to breathe.

How I keep writing that.

"Did anyone ever tell you that you look just like Shirley Temple?" His arms snaking around her, his hand over her mouth, her nose. "You know how Shirley Temple got famous? I'll make you famous."

How I keep writing about her abduction, rape, attempted murder in what is now a park beside the river near my house where I cycle and walk along the riverbank, through the trees. The ripple of light recalling the light rippling her eyes as he dragged her along the rocky bank. Her child voice calling for her mother. Her mother's voice calling her from the river.

How I keep writing what she looked like when she escaped his death blow with a rock, plunged into the river, a tiny, skinny, half-naked, beaten, bitten child of eleven, started knocking on doors and the doors kept closing until an older woman pulled her inside, wrapped her in a quilt, rocked her, called the police, repeated over and over, "This is not your fault. You did nothing wrong."

How I keep writing that my mother's boned-down, oxygen-starved mother comforted her. Died three weeks later at forty-six. Keep writing how her sister, who became her caretaker, died of meningitis one year later. Keep writing how my mother escaped her alcoholic father's abuse at thirteen, spent the rest of her life looking after herself, her family, friends, strangers, even as she lay dying.

How I keep writing and often can't write about what it means to be a woman looking—being looked at, doing the looking, looking out, looking after, living long enough to see children grow up, to wear time in our bodies, our faces, our minds.

| She always wore lipstick. Usually red, though at times she experimented with the hues of the era—pale pinks and beiges, eggplant purple, orange coral. And eyebrow pencil— a brown arch over her eyes dark green as the forest, the river. The care she gave her hair—permed or straight, curled or backcombed, hairdresser cut or barbered, blonde or brown, and once, when she dyed it at our home in the mountains— flaming, fluorescent orange, and she threw on a diaphanous purple scarf, traversed the wind uptown to the store where my father worked as a butcher and he looked up from behind the meat counter, "Jesus Christ."

Even when she was suffering advanced lung disease, the only one of eight siblings to live past seventy. Could barely get up off her couch in her tiny subsidized apartment in the city she'd moved back to, and she'd greet us from her couch, bloom of bruises on her face and neck from the oxygen cannula, down her arms, her skin thinned by steroids and oxygen starvation. Her red lips, arched eyebrows. Her undyed brown hair grown out of the barber cut she loved, thinned and swooped up the back of her head, too sick to tolerate the odours a hairdresser would bring into her apartment, so I and my nieces cut her hair, and when that was too much, my nieces tenderly stroked her head, "You look beautiful to us, Gramma," made pictures and videos of her and them and my sister, their hair done up wild, lips flaming red, smiling, laughing, making exaggerated faces.

Her hand in mine on the couch as she turned to look at me, and I want to write in the present tense, *turns to look*, so that she can still be seeing, so that she can read what I am writing the way she read everything I wrote about her.

"You look better like that," she said/says, "lipstick gives you a little colour, makes you look more alive."

And I looked/look at her and my heart breaks for her suffering, her desire to ease our suffering with her red lips and arched brows, her vulnerable toughness, her desire to protect us, the often-brutal complexities of being a woman in a culture that defines and values us by our looks.

| The power that is conferred on women by fashion, culture, corporate interests, religion, but has nothing to do with who we are.

The power that feels like power as long as we look as if we're trying. As if looks are a moral issue.

The power that can turn into rage against us. At any age.

The power that strives to turn us into play dolls, trophy partners, hot bitches, charity doyennes, patriarchy mouth-pieces, used-up hags.

The power that is age denying and illusive, disguises itself as love, admiration, fear.

The power that asks for and rewards needles in the face, cut flesh, abraded flesh, bruised swelling, Barbie-doll pouty lips, frozen foreheads, plastic cheeks, round eyes in perpetually baby-doll eerie vacant gazes.

The power that has nothing to do with the will, the ability, the courage to do. To think. To be.

The power that threatens us with sexualized violence, irrelevance, and invisibility, keeps us striving, paying, dancing on the head of a pin, dying to admit it, turning inside out in denial.

The power that can be a relief and a danger to have. To lose.

The power that is racialized, binary, heteronormative, class based.

The power that can go all poor me, bare its fists, guns, knives, teeth, pricks, when called out or challenged.

The power that eats its daughters, tells us to try harder, be more grateful.

The power that threatens us if we leave home.

Those of us who've had a home.

| We are/were in the sun beside the river, my mom and me, across from the park where people come to picnic, play games, splash in the river, walk their dogs, cycle.

Just upriver of where she was raped, beaten, bitten, where she crossed and started banging on doors.

Several kilometres upriver from her childhood home— an unpainted clapboard house across from the train yards that the owner of a trucking company kindly let her and her seven siblings, mother and father live in because two of her brothers drove truck for him.

The clapboard where her mother, who often told my mother that she was French, very French, curled her black hair with an iron heated on the wood'n coal stove, reddened her oxygen-starved lips, sewed dresses and shirts and pants for herself and her children. Donned a dress, high-heeled boots, a jaunty hat to walk to the shops to buy food. When she wasn't in bed, unable to breathe. When she wasn't being beaten by her blond, drunk, English-born husband.

The clapboard where my mother's brothers teased her about her big lips—threatened to lick them and stick her to the wall. Where her mother comforted her—"consider the source"—when kids taunted her—"Evelyn Morris, Evelyn Morris, more ass and tits than anything else."

Where her father's words, sometimes fists, drove into her head—"you look like your mother, you should have died instead."

We are/were in the park downriver from the shack on the outer edge of the city where her father moved her and her brother after their mother died. Where he tried to trade her for a case of beer to one of his drinking buddies, tried to rape her except for her beloved thirteen-year-old brother who happened to be there, held their father off with a rifle.

We are/were downriver from the shack next door to hers where she made friends with a young couple, babysat their baby daughter, and the man treated the woman with love and respect, and they both talked openly about the woman having been a prostitute during the war when she lived with her mother and sisters because she could make enough money to help buy food, pay rent.

The shack where my mother is a traumatized child the
doctors have told is so damaged inside that she'll never have
children, where she can't imagine the future she will live
into, her lungs as ravaged as her dead mother's, her children
looking after her in her seniors' subsidized apartment, and
an old man will move into her building and she will tell him
he looks familiar, like a man who lived in a shack near hers,
whose wife had been a prostitute, and they will figure out
that the young lovers are his brother and sister-in-law, and
my mother will tell him she'd wanted to die with her mother,
they helped save her life with their unconditional love and
friendship, and he will tell her he remembers them talking
about the little girl in the shack next door.

Her river eyes will flash as she tells me how her neighbour
in her seniors' building said that his brother and sister-in-law
loved each other with that same unconditional love until the
day they died.

Her eyes flash as we sat/sit downriver from the shack my
mother left after her father beat her so badly she could hardly
walk, moved in with one of her five brothers—the one most
like their father—and his wife. Babysat her nephews, helped
out, until her brother tried to rape her in a drunken rage
against his wife.

We are/were upriver from the downtown core, the glass
towers glowing, the jail cell that no longer exists in their
shadows where she was locked up for a week because she
kept evading the authorities who wanted to put her in a home
for "incorrigibles," place her back in her father's or violent
brother's care, and so she kept running.

She and another teenaged girl in the jail cell talked about
what they were running from, their survival options—
hooking, waitressing, laundry work, farm work. Lying about
their age. Leaving town.

She ran when they let her out—to BC to work on a farm, to the hospital in Banff to work as an aide, to the Brewster hotel to work in the basement laundry, back to Calgary to waitress in various cafes. And for a year a refugee couple from worn-torn Europe took her in, taught her to cook, bank, experience a safe home.

Beside the river we are/were smelling the wind blowing over the mountains. Even with the oxygen cannula in her nostrils she can/could smell rain or snow on the wind. Just as she could in our old miner's house in the Crowsnest Pass that she focussed her uncanny energy on. Painted and wall-papered so that we never knew what the walls would be like when we came home, removed the shingles and roof herself, knocked out walls, removed and replaced windows, replaced doors, cleaned with a vengeance against poverty, cooked for the friends and strangers who came almost every day to shoot the shit, play in my dad's band, or were running away from violence and trauma.

Beside the river she is in her wheelchair, the wheelchair that I take her in to medical appointments, out for lunch, around the neighbourhood where we live two blocks apart. The wheelchair my twin nieces and sister, who are part of our caretaking team, push her in beside the river so that she can watch birds, dogs, talk with children, throw a ball the way she did when she was young and a wicked pitcher. Until the three years when she can no longer leave her apartment and my sister and nieces and I come to her. Self-conscious about the bruises under her thin skin, her inability to get up, cook, clean, her lack of muscle, she greets us from the couch with lipstick and eyebrow pencil, "how the hell are you."

That day, those days, beside the river, there are/were just the two of us. We have come from a hearing clinic where the audiologist, a woman younger than my mom and me, spoke loud enough for my mom to hear, listened to my exuberant mom—as gaunt and hollow cheeked in her wheelchair as her oxygen-starved mom in photos—green eyes flashing, hands flying—tell stories about playing baseball until she was forty-eight and cleated so hard by an opposing player that one of her ribs snapped, sliced her lung and it collapsed, and she spent weeks in hospital with tubes stuck through her ribs draining bloody fluid into a bottle, and the audiologist, also exuberant and straightforward, didn't patronize either of us.

The fact that I should note that—the freedom from being patronized, cutified, young ladied.

And how I, in my sixties, even though I have thought and talked and written about the toxic blend of sexism and ageism, wrestle with the yoke, the burden, the double standard of "likability" that we place on women. Is she/was she, nice enough, too nice, taking up too much space, too loud, too quiet, too ambitious, too strong, too weak, too headstrong, acting her age, dressing her age, making an effort, making too much of an effort, too controlling, too uncontrolled, pleasing enough to look at, sexy enough, too sexy, too aggressive, too pushy, too weak, too powerful, too young, too old.

The yoke, the burden, the stricture that gets applied to women and girls in public and in private. That we internalize before we know we are internalizing it. That is deeply implicit in democracies that would sooner elect blatant lying, racist, homophobic, sexist, autocratic, dangerous, narcissistic men than a woman, any woman, no matter how qualified. That gets applied to women premiers in Canada, prevents more women from becoming premiers, while too many of their male counterparts get away with lying, bullying, cheating, dividing, boasting, decimating public health care and education while they boost their wealthy cronies. The stricture that is the stark and ugly truth behind women still making less than our male counterparts, still getting fewer promotions, still needing to watch where and how we walk, what and how we talk.

Beside the river we are/were eating a treat from Angel's Cafe. My mom sips coffee, chews on her sweet treat, a hat pulled jaunty over her brow, sun glinting off the clear cord running from the oxygen tank on the back of her wheelchair, up her neck to the cannula in her flared nostrils. Her breath is/was shallow, laboured.

I divide my attention between watching and listening— past, present, and future—the hollowness of her cheeks, the bruises from the cord on her face, her neck, the thinness of her hands, the battered little girl deathly afraid of water plunging into the river to escape a murderous man, the woman who could hit home runs out of any ball park, opened her home in the mountains to strangers who needed food/ shelter, the woman who took on the government for a sewage lagoon stinking up the mountain valley where she used to live, the traumatized girl who wanted to die when they told her that her mother had died, the young woman who went to her dying father's bedside and told him that she forgave him, the woman who nursed two of her brothers when they were dying, babysat six grandchildren, took them swimming, camping, picked them up after school, picked them up and hugged them when they were afraid, cold-cocked a man who groped her, rode horses through the mountains here and in Australia where she took a job in her fifties guiding tourists, fed people in her subsidized seniors' apartment building, drove them to medical appointments, helped them apply for Aids for Daily Living, until she no longer could.

And I was/am thinking about something that my sister and her twin daughters who visited my mother, cooked for and ate with her almost every day for three years often say—no matter how fragile Gramma got physically, she was an incredibly strong person.

And beside the river I ask/asked her, as I often did, "Where do you get the strength, Mom?"

And she cocked her head, the way she did/does, "From my mom. She was a skinny, sick little woman, but she knew how to care. Everyone loved her, you would have too."

Swig of her coffee, her laboured breath, bruised hands, hollowed cheeks. "Don't feel sorry for me, Bert. I've had a good life."

| When she was in her seventies and still driving, still swaggery, still taking people from her building to medical appointments, looking after her brother who died of the same lung disease that she will/did die from.

She and her sister-in-law in an auto service centre for her sister-in-law's car. Something simple, like an oil change or regular service. My mom who read her manual inside out, knew her own car inside out.

Waited for hours, while other people came and went.

The answers she got from the men at the counter—"yours will be up next. Don't worry, ladies, we'll have you out of here soon." Mostly nothing—no acknowledgements, no explanations. As if they weren't there, had become invisible, their time unimportant.

Until my mom swaggered to the counter. "You're keeping us waiting because you think we're a couple of little old ladies, don't you?"

And the man blushed, started to protest, and my mom put up her hand. "Well we're not, we're a couple of little old men in drag."

| And yet.

Even so.

Still.

Despite "looks are skin deep."

Despite years of analysis about the objectification of women and girls.

Despite the years and changes since the fifties when the Western world threw money and propaganda at women after the war telling us/them that androgyny was no longer valued, that high heels and sexualized clothing were what "real" women desired, needed, would be valued for. No matter that it's impossible to run in heels, you'll have to rely on feminine wile, so don't worry your pretty little head, you'll never have too much power.

Especially if you're not lily-of-the-valley white, starvation thin, botoxed, siliconed, dyed, blow dried, heterosexual, able bodied, young, trying to look young, dying to look young, moneyed, moneyed looking, following the money, honey.

| Because women generally have less money as we enter "retirement."

Because, according to the US Institute for Women's Policy Research, "longitudinal dataset showing total earnings over the most recent 15 years for all workers who worked in at least one year showed women workers faced an actual gap of 51% in the 2001–2015 time period."

Because women tend to be marginalized and diminished on the job as we age, while men are considered more valuable and competent, despite the pattern that Angela Duckworth notes in her book, *Grit*: women's grit increases with age, our "ambition begins to increase after 55 and peaks after 65."

Because, according to the US National Bureau of Economic Research, resumés of older women get far fewer call backs than those of older men and younger applicants of either sex.

Because of the sexist lie that we have drunk for far too long: "Men age like a glass of wine, women like a glass of milk."

Because there is solidarity and strength in pouring this lie down the drain.

| I was forty-five, the streak of silver in my hair widening. A casual comment by a young store clerk when I was shopping for shoes with my sister-in-law who is ten years younger than me, colours her hair to hide the grey. "Ah," the clerk smiled at us, "a mother and daughter out shopping."

An external, casual remark, and I bought a box of hair dye, close to the colour my hair used to be in the days when I would ask hairdressers to cut my hair in a style that made me look older, because people thought I was way younger than I was and often talked down to me. Dark chocolate brown with auburn lights.

Over dinner one of my six-year-old nieces kept staring at me, finally nodded as if she'd figured something out, "Auntie Berta, now that you dyed your hair, you look a lot younger. Except your face."

| Despite growing up in poverty, particularly until the age of ten, with many of the traumas and insecurities that come with poverty—uncertain food and shelter, frequent moves, a stint of homelessness, physical and emotional stress—
I live with many of the privileges society bestows on certain people. I am white, middle class, non-disabled, live in a heterosexual relationship, went to university when it was affordable for working-class kids, experienced the power of being what is considered an attractive young woman. The

effects of trauma, both intergenerational and personal—
bouts of depression and anxiety, anorexia in my youth,
excessive worry about people I love, a tendency to shame
myself with harsh self-judgement, a frugality that borders on
cheapness—are mostly hidden.

While I don't often get told that I look good for my age, I
am often told that something particular looks good—my hair,
which is grey; the way a scarf a friend gave me looks; the way
I free dance in my workout class; something that I'm wearing.
Mostly I enjoy these affirmations, though I have to work at it,
as I'm inclined to feel embarrassed by attention, good or bad,
even when I crave some good attention.

And while I like to play with coloured scarves, glasses,
shirts, boots, lip gloss, I'm not inclined to dye my hair, wear
much makeup, silicone my lips, botox my face.

Since my mother's death and the deaths of close friends,
I'm more inclined to think of how I want to spend energy in
whatever time I have left on this earth. So far none of these
activities compel me to botox, surgery, or silicone injections.

Mostly I want to strive to be as honest, creative, courageous as women of all ages who have worked hard on issues
I think are important—social justice, racism, sexism, ageism,
climate change, gender equity, poverty reduction, fair trade.

When I find myself struggling with internalized sexism/
ageism—is my writing still relevant, what's the point in writing
about these things, what's the point in writing at all—I look
to writers of my generation and generations older for wisdom
and inspiration, am moved to my knees at the humanity in
the words of women writing from the perspective of age
and experience.

| According to my mom and her brothers, their mother—
when she wasn't bedridden with asthma—used to garden

and cook for her eight hungry children, frequently leave a pie "cooling" on the windowsill so that homeless people riding the rails during the '30s could take it without having to feel like charity cases. When she was dying, she sewed clothing for her children, one of her last acts.

According to family narrative and photos, their mother came as a child by covered wagon from North Dakota where she was born, with five siblings and her French-speaking parents, homesteaded in southern Alberta near Medicine Hat. She married an English-born, Sidney Mines–raised man with very white skin, sober charm, violent alcoholism, had nine children. My mom was the second youngest, a tiny, tawny-skinned, fiercely loving child.

When my mom's oldest brother died he had a smudging ceremony at the Calgary Native Friendship Centre. His son had married a Cree woman, and one of his sisters had married a man from Lac la Biche who, people whispered, was "Indian," words never spoken out loud.

After the smudge I asked the elder how well he knew my uncle. He said that he knew him very well; my uncle came to the Friendship Centre every day. I asked him if he knew why my uncle came to the centre every day, and he said that I should talk to my family.

The two uncles I asked about this told me not to bring these things up. When they were dying they both told me that their mother was Métis but wouldn't say anything more. When I talked with my cousin, whose father had the smudge, he told me that he'd known since he was sixteen.

I have no proof that this is true, no proof that it isn't. I cannot claim Métis identity, as I knew nothing about the possibility until I was in my forties, have experienced none of the culture nor any of the racism.

Why do I mention this in a piece on looking good for your age?

As my mom sickened, she came to look more like the child who'd been abducted, raped, and tortured. As I was looking after her she would sometimes call me "Mom," then, "I know you're not my mom, but sometimes you look like her, except you're pale."

A month before she died I went to the *Walking with Our Sisters* exhibit in Calgary, told the elder who smudged me in, gave me the red tobacco bundle to take with me as I walked along the river of moccasin vamps representing the Missing and Murdered Aboriginal Girls and Women, that I am the daughter of a woman who survived abduction, rape, and attempted murder. She hugged me, told me to either leave my bundle beside a pair of vamps decorated by the families of the missing girls and women, or bring it back along with the tissues she gave me for tears, and she would burn them at the teepee ceremony in the evening.

Home in her tiny subsidized apartment, fighting for breath, my mom walked with me along this river of missing girls and women, as I stopped and whispered to each pair of vamps, listening for the pair that would ask me to leave my red-tied tobacco bundle. I couldn't stop crying for all of these girls and women, wishing that the river could run backward and they could all rise upriver, walk safely back to their loved ones.

And then there they were. One vamp with a woman beaded from the back, a little girl beside her, leaning into her. On the other vamp another girl, bigger than the little girl. Shaking so hard I thought I would dissolve, I lay the bundle beside these vamps.

I told the elder who smudged me out that I had left my tobacco bundle beside a pair of vamps that told a story similar to my mom's. She also hugged me tight, said that she would tell my mom's story at that evening's teepee ceremony. I told her that my mom was very sick, could I take her a tobacco bundle, and she smudged me one, told me to tell my mom to hold it and think about her mom and sister and pray, then take it out to a clean place in Nature and release the tobacco. I said that my mom could no longer go out, could family do it, and she said that we could.

When I gave my mom the bundle she seemed skeptical, but the next day she told me she'd been holding the bundle and sleeping with it, had started seeing her mom and sister. I asked her how she felt, and she said she liked seeing them, maybe it meant she was dying.

The evening she was rushed into hospital she joked with the nurse who was sticking electrodes to her chest, "You're doing that because you wanted to see my tits, didn't you," and he laughed, and later she asked me to give him chocolate for being so good to her.

So sick she couldn't eat, go to the toilet, the third-last day of her life, she asked me to talk to one of her three room-mates because he was upset that his daughter just found out she carried the Huntington's gene that was killing him. She asked me to share chocolate with him, comfort one of her other roommates who was distressed because she couldn't find her mother. Then she put her hand out to me, "Hold my hand, Bert, don't leave me."

The day before she died she was moved to a private room, and members of our family stayed with her to try to comfort her—through the day and through the night. Three of my nieces sat beside her all night, moved down the bed when I came back in from a few hours at home, "She's waiting for you, she wants you."

No longer able to speak, she gazed into my eyes for three hours as I whispered, "You can do it, you can make it," echoing what she'd told me a vision of her mom had said when my mom was young and I was a baby and she'd technically died and thought she heard her mother calling her from on top of a hill, even though it was a resident doing CPR, and she said it was that and seeing me as a baby on her chest that brought her back.

I hoped she was comforted by what I was saying, that maybe she thought I was her mother or her sister and she was going toward them.

For the last half hour, she focussed on my mouth.

Until her last breath.

| Before my mother died, a woman I know who is status said that her family would like her to pass as white, since she's pale skinned, because it's safer to be a white woman or girl, safer in every way—from the dangers that threaten Indigenous girls and women in our society to the dangers that threaten Indigenous people in educational, legal, police, and health-care systems.

I'd written fiction from the point of view of my grandmother having her youngest daughter brought home beaten beyond recognition, so traumatized that the only person she could bear was her mother. I'd tried to imagine what it must have been like for my grandmother to know that she herself was dying and leaving her traumatized child. I wrote these stories before my uncles told me their mother was Métis. It was only after my mother died that I began to imagine what it must have been like for my grandmother if what my uncles said was true. Why did she tell her sons, but not her youngest daughter? Did she tell her two older daughters? If she didn't tell her youngest daughter as an attempt to protect her from the violence perpetrated on Indigenous and Métis girls and women, what must she have gone through in those three weeks before her death?

Whether or not it's true that my grandmother was Métis, the humanity, the generosity of the elders for my mom, for me—a pale white woman—bearing my mother's story, fills me with gratitude, humility, awe.

The day after my mom died I found the red tobacco bundle under my mom's pillow in her apartment. Raw, grieving, we went as a family to the place beside the river where she emerged as a beaten child.

Together we crossed the river to the place where the man tried to murder her, stood in a circle. I opened the red bundle and each of her four children, six grandchildren, took some tobacco, held it in our palms, walked among the trees and stones until we found a clean spot.

Scent of tobacco.

Pines and spruce.

River.

Her green eyes, no matter how young, how old, how sick, how healthy.

That fierce love.

Her mother and sister waiting for her on the other side.

The friends and families of all the murdered and missing women and girls.

Calling their names.

Calling them.

Upriver.

Into their longing arms.

Into a future when they can trace the lines of time, of age, in their loved ones' faces, "you are beautiful, so so beautiful."

Help Fund Pam's Vital Medical Procedure

OLYN OZBICK

@HRHPamela Click HERE to support my important KICKFUNDSTER campaign called **PAM's VITAL MEDICAL LINEAMENT PROCEDURE** 😘

10 hours ago   2 people like this   0 shares

@Liz_Laugh_Luv Oh noooooooo! Poor sweeeeet Pammmy 💕 Are you okay? I'll bring you lasagna.

9 hours ago   6 people like this   2 shares

@HRHPamela The procedure is amazing 😊 A breakthrough, really. And I am in dire need of it 😘

9 hours ago   2 people like this   3 shares

@Liz_Laugh_Luv I'm sooooo sad you need this 💔 What happened? Are you up to talking? Should I bring soup instead 💕💕

9 hours ago   2 people like this   0 shares

73

@HRHPamela I just feel it's time. I've put it off too long because I really can't afford it 💸 But now it's really essential. Please help by clicking my KICKFUNDSTER link.

9 hours ago   5 people like this   3 shares

@Kim_Cougar_atPlay OMG I'm so excited!!! A KICKFUNDSTER!!!! Good for you Pam!!!! What exactly is wrong?????? Soooooo wanting this to be a success for you!!!

9 hours ago   2 people like this   0 shares

@HRHPamela It's an expensive procedure 🤑 💵 But what would you expect for such vital medical intervention! Click the KICKFUNDSTER link and I'll love you forever 😘

9 hours ago   2 people like this   0 shares

@Kim_Cougar_atPlay AMAZING!!!! What exactly is a Linament, Pam? It sounds SO SERIOUS!!!!!

9 hours ago   2 people like this   0 shares

@Spawn_of_HRH A lineament is a face. My Mom wants a facelift. She says she NEEDS it. Personally, I don't think she does at all. She's completely gorgeous 🦢 and not just for her age. Love ya Mom, inside and out!

9 hours ago   2 people like this   0 shares

@Kim_Cougar_atPlay OMG Pam, I agree. I don't think you need this at ALLLL!!!! Maybe in another three years! MAYBE!!!!!! You're actually SO!!!!!! Gorgeous!!! You're AMAZING!!!!! And not just for your age!!!

9 hours ago   2 people like this   0 shares

@HRHPamela   Does that mean you won't contribute to my **VITAL MEDICAL LINEAMENT PROCEDURE.** KICKFUNDSTER 😨 I wish you would 😩 I really want it 😬

9 hours ago   2 people like this   0 shares

@Liz_Laugh_Luv   Uhmmmm! Soooooo! There's nothing actually WRONG with you Pam 🖤💔 You don't really neeeeed this?

9 hours ago   8 people like this   2 shares

@Angel(a)_Face   LET ME SEE if I've I got things right here. With this KICKFUNDSTER, you FAIL to BUDGET correctly for YOURSELF and then people BUY YOU things?

9 hours ago   5 people like this   0 shares

@Liz_Laugh_Luv   Aw Jen, you don't need a face lift 💔👧 Your daughter is right! You are sooooo beautiful 🙀

9 hours ago   6 people like this   3 shares

@Angel(a)_Face   And on TOP of NOT BUDGETING correctly, is it possible this is also a result of Pam being GUILTY of EXFOLIATING INCORRECTLY!?

9 hours ago   6 people like this   1 shares

@Liz_Laugh_Luv   I agreeeee! Proper exfoliating never hurts. It enhances your natural beauty. Maybe you could do just a bit more at home, but why would you think you need face surgery lovely Pammy 💋

9 hours ago   2 people like this   0 shares

@HRHPamela I just think people don't see me as someone special anymore. I don't want to be just an old lady. I don't want to stop being special. It's time to admit I'm getting old 👓

9 hours ago   2 people like this   0 shares

@Liz_Laugh_Luv Stop that right nowwwwww! If you think you are old, you will go running down that road faster than a rabbit in front of a truck 🐰 But if you know you are beautiful then that is what you will be! And you ARE so beautiful Pammmy! **Gorgeoussssss! Amazzzzzing! Beautifuuuuul! You always have been and we luvvvv you** ❤️❤️❤️ MWAH 👄

9 hours ago   2 people like this   0 shares

@Angel(a)_Face I might support this dubious process but UNFORTUNATELY, I've just spent $1000 on my Golden Retriever's kidney treatment. OUT OF MY OWN POCKET— WOAH (I know you might have to sit down to take that in.)

9 hours ago   7 people like this   0 shares

@HRHPamela Dogs are expensive 😱 I spent $200 on my dog this week.

9 hours ago   2 people like this   0 shares

@Liz_Laugh_Luv Oh nooooo! What's wrong with sweet Mugsy 🐱 🐱 How can I help?

9 hours ago   6 people like this   0 shares

@HRHPamela Walk her sometime 😚 That would be a huge help.

9 hours ago   2 people like this   0 shares

@Liz_Laugh_Luv   Ohhhhhh goooood 😻 So she can still walk
then 🐩

8 hours ago   5 people like this   0 shares

@HRHPamela   Of course she can walk 👌 She can run, she's
a Spaniel 😃

8 hours ago   5 people like this   0 shares

@Liz_Laugh_Luv   Yaaaaay hooorayyyy 💜 Then why did she
go to the vet?

8 hours ago   0 people like this   0 shares

@HRHPamela   Dog spa. Grooming 🐑

8 hours ago   5 people like this   0 shares

@Liz_Laugh_Luv   Hmmm. At least *she looks good* 🐩 ‼️

8 hours ago   6 people like this   3 shares

@HRHPamela   Tuesday at 5 would be great for the walk
'cause I'm out for drinks with the girls then 😜

8 hours ago   6 people like this   3 shares

@Liz_Laugh_Luv   The girls? Whaaaat girls?

8 hours ago   0 people like this   0 shares

@HRHPamela   Angie and Kim. We do cocktails 😊 🍸 🍸 on
Tuesdays.

8 hours ago   2 people like this   0 shares

@Liz_Laugh_Luv   Niiiiiice 😼 Let me get this straight. Mugsy
can walk. You can talk. And you do cocktails without me.
Good for you all 💔

8 hours ago   1 people like this   0 shares

@HRHPamela   So, Tuesday 😬

8 hours ago   2 people like this   0 shares

@Liz_Laugh_Luv   Absoluuuuutely not.

8 hours ago   8 people like this   0 shares

@HRHPamela   But I can count on your donation 😬

8 hours ago   0 people like this   0 shares

@Liz_Laugh_Luv   You should set up a KICKFUNDSTER for
the gin and tonic bill 🍸 🖤

7 hours ago   27 people like this   1 shares

@HRHPamela   I don't drink gin 😆

7 hours ago   2 people like this   13 shares

@Angel(a)_Face   Pam wouldn't need MEDICALLY
ENHANCED YOUTHFULNESS if she'd started looking after
herself 20 years ago. I was always telling her **STAY OUT OF
THE SUN.**

7 hours ago   27 people like this   3 shares

@Kim_Cougar_atPlay   BAHHAHA!!!!! That's right!!!! It's not
up to us to pay for the mistakes of her youth!! HA!!!!!!

7 hours ago   6 people like this   0 shares

@Angel(a)_Face   CORRECT ✔ We are all too busy paying
for the MISTAKES of our OWN YOUTH.

7 hours ago   8 people like this   3 shares

@Liz_Laugh_Luv Don't listen to them Pammy. You're beautiful. Just keep thinking that, because it's true. You don't have to beeee old if you don't thiiiiink you are.

7 hours ago   2 people like this   0 shares

@HRHPamela Darling Lizzy, I need you to stop YOUR way of thinking. I'm not beautiful, I need this treatment. Don't talk yourself or the others out of this. I want my funding.

7 hours ago   2 people like this   0 shares

@Kim_Cougar_atPlay HAHA!!!!! This would be a lot cheaper for all of us if you handled things Lizzies way!!! Ignore your age and it will go AWAYYYY!!! BAHA!!!!

7 hours ago   2 people like this   0 shares

@HRHPamela But where do you draw the line 😕 We live in a country where our taxes pay each other's hip replacements. Each other's hearing aids. Why not face enhancements?

7 hours ago   2 people like this   0 shares

@Angel(a)_Face I'm NOT paying for your hearing aids too Pam. You WRECKED your ears with your TERRIBLE music back in the 90s! I KNEW this was coming.

7 hours ago   3 people like this   0 shares

@HRHPamela Owwwww. My feelings are 💔 now. I guess I'll have to take advantage of my Canadian health care 🏥 and get my emotions checked now, too. Thanks for paying taxes everyone!

7 hours ago   2 people like this   2 shares

@Angel(a)_Face   You're WELCOME 🙏 I'm STARTING to SEE how this works. We really shouldn't have to plan ahead to pay for ANYTHING.

7 hours ago   5 people like this   2 share

@Kim_Cougar_atPlay   OMG too funny!!!! Who wants to go out and buy me dinner tonight??? I forgot to plan to feed myself in my senior years! Now I'm always hungry!!!

7 hours ago   10 people like this   4 shares

@HRHPamela   You're not senior, you're fifty 🐣 What are you going to do when you're actually old Kim? Start planning now 🤔

7 hours ago   6 people like this   0 shares

@Kim_Cougar_atPlay   OMG I am already soooooo planning, haha!!!!!!! I have a complex KICKFUNDSTER in development to take me well into my nineties!

7 hours ago   7 people like this   1 shares

@Liz_Laugh_Luv   I'll come with you Kim, if no one else wants to 🍰🍩

7 hours ago   2 people like this   0 shares

@Angel(a)_Face   I hope Kim has included EXFOLIATION expenses in her plan. NO ONE wants to see a WOMAN PAST FIFTY who hasn't afforded expensive SCRUBS.

7 hours ago   2 people like this   1 shares

@Kim_Cougar_atPlay   BAAHAHA!!!! Of course!!!!! And oysters!!!! I'm planning several Oyster Fund Me's!!!

7 hours ago   10 people like this   2 shares

@Liz_Laugh_Luv Oysters, yuk

7 hours ago   6 people like this   0 shares

@Kim_Cougar_atPlay   HAHAA!!! Dear Liz!!! We must attend to the future of our sex-drives!!!!! I'll launch a Sexy-Sex-Drive Fund Me for you. It'll be Amazzzing!!! I think you could use it.

7 hours ago   7 people like this   2 shares

@Angel(a)_Face   Liz needs a SEX DRIVE like the Boy Scouts need a BOTTLE DRIVE.

7 hours ago   20 people like this   1 shares

@HRHPamela   OR....maybe if Liz ignores sex it will go away

7 hours ago   42 people like this   12 shares

@Kim_Cougar_atPlay   It will! HEEHEE!!! I can attest to that! Ignore sex and it WILL go away.

7 hours ago   22 people like this   10 shares

@Angel(a)_Face   So, if we EXTRAPOLATE from here then, maybe Liz is CORRECT about AGING also. Let's all IGNORE it.

7 hours ago   2 people like this   0 shares

@Kim_Cougar_atPlay   OMG I'm dying!!!!! Don't listen to Angela, Liz. What you need is a Boy Scout!!! Well, not a boy, that's disgusting. A Man Scout. A young man to scout out your needs haaaa haaaa!!!!!

7 hours ago   5 people like this   0 shares

@Liz_Laugh_Luv   I don't have sex problems. I am sexy

7 hours ago   9 people like this   0 shares

@Angel(a)_Face SURE YOU ARE dear, and we want you to KEEP THINKING that way.

7 hours ago   12 people like this   4 shares

@Liz_Laugh_Luv Please stop 'dearing' me. I 🖤🖤 you all, but I think that's patronizing. Matronizing? Anyway, it's condescending 🪥 And insulting 😡

7 hours ago   2 people like this   0 shares

@Kim_Cougar_atPlay Ooooooohh!!!! You've hurt Lizzies feelings again!!!

6 hours ago   2 people like this   0 shares

@Liz_Laugh_Luv Just 🖤🙏 don't start a Sex Drive Fund Me for me!

6 hours ago   12 people like this   5 shares

@HRHPamela Let's refocus on the donations, DEARS 😚 Can I count on all of you to contribute 😉

6 hours ago   2 people like this   0 shares

@Liz_Laugh_Luv Pammmy luv! 🖤 You should use all this energy toward something else. I really don't like conversations about getting old. People start this kind of talk in their 30s and it just gets worse. I hate to indulge it! 👧 💔 You talk old...you think old...you get old...

6 hours ago   2 people like this   0 shares

@Angel(a)_Face RIGHT and look at our Lizzy now, SEXY young thing!

6 hours ago   2 people like this   0 shares

@Liz_Laugh_Luv Yes ‼️ I ‼️ Ammmm ‼️
6 hours ago   2 people like this   0 shares

@Kim_Cougar_atPlay   OMG!!!! Do you talk a lot about sex,
Lizzy????? Is that what made you so sexy?????
6 hours ago   2 people like this   0 shares

@Angel(a)_Face   INQUIRING MINDS want to know!
6 hours ago   2 people like this   0 shares

@Liz_Laugh_Luv   Now you're just making fun of me 💔
6 hours ago   2 people like this   0 shares

@Angel(a)_Face   Okay, CHANGING subject. I UNDERSTAND
why Pam needs help. I pretty much SUCKED at LIFE when I
was young and I'm paying for it now also.
6 hours ago   6 people like this   1 shares

@HRHPamela   Owww, I've never sucked at life 🙁
6 hours ago   6 people like this   0 shares

@Kim_Cougar_atPlay   OMG I'm dying!!!!! 👏 👏 👏
6 hours ago   2 people like this   0 shares

@Liz_Laugh_Luv   I don't want you to take this wrong Pam
🐾 You know how much we all luvvvv you 💚 🐱 But you
might want to use a bit of the money for fixing your life not
your face. Just a kind suggestion, truly. From your caring
friends 💋
5 hours ago   8 people like this   2 shares

@HRHPamela   Because none of you lovely ladies have donated a penny, where the money is going is a non-issue so 😘 🐷

5 hours ago   6 people like this   0 shares

@Angel(a)_Face   Just putting this out there

5 hours ago   6 people like this   2 shares

@HRHPamela   I'll consider that my first donation 😊 🙏
5 hours ago   2 people like this   0 shares

@Kim_Cougar_atPlay   Yummmmmm!!!! Looks moist!
5 hours ago   5 people like this   3 shares

@Liz_Laugh_Luv   Ugh, stop 🖤 🤢
5 hours ago   6 people like this   0 shares

@Kim_Cougar_atPlay   HEEHEEEE!!! Liz is one of those people who hates the word moiiiist heee!!!
5 hours ago   11 people like this   0 shares

@HRHPamela   Grow up, Liz, you are a fifty year old woman There is nothing gross about the word moist.
5 hours ago   12 people like this   3 shares

@Angel(a)_Face   Yes, don't be a FRUITCAKE.
5 hours ago   6 people like this   0 shares

@Liz_Laugh_Luv 🗿 ✋

5 hours ago   2 people like this   0 shares

@Kim_Cougar_atPlay   Heeeheee!!! Lizeeee!!!! 🦁 ☁

5 hours ago   2 people like this   0 shares

@HRHPamela   Enough 🐃 💩 You should all fund this facial procedure.

5 hours ago   3 people like this   1 shares

@Angel(a)_Face   I am starting to QUESTION whether making Pam (and Liz) comfortable by fixing their faces (and avoiding the word MOIST) is really MY RESPONSIBLITY.

4 hours ago   4 people like this   1 shares

@Liz_Laugh_Luv   Maybe a meditation course would be a good plan for you, Pam. 🐵 Or use your KICKFUNDSTER to travel to a Buddhist monastery 🙏

4 hours ago   2 people like this   0 shares

@Angel(a)_Face   Whatever she decides, Pam should start home treatments now, like the rest of us did IN OUR TEENS. I know drying egg whites on my face made me feel I was ALL GROWN UP and PREPARING for a responsible ADULT future the way I was EXPECTED to.

4 hours ago   6 people like this   0 shares

@Kim_Cougar_atPlay   HAAA!!! But that would require her to spend time actually doing something!!!! BAH!!

4 hours ago   2 people like this   3 shares

@HRHPamela   I would like to point out that I am fully adult.

4 hours ago   7 people like this   2 shares

@Angel(a)_Face   I think Pam should have PLANNED for making a proper LIVING so she could afford the THINGS SHE NEEDED in life. Maybe a good EDUCATION and a good JOB would have been a better use of her YOUTHFUL PLANNING.

4 hours ago   5 people like this   0 shares

@HRHPamela   Seems like it's time to share some of this

4 hours ago   6 people like this   0 shares

@Kim_Cougar_atPlay   EEEKK!!!! But what about her faaaace???? If she'd gone into The Sciences, her face would still be drooping, and she would still be trying to fund her expensive Facial Procedure!!!!!

4 hours ago   2 people like this ·   3 shares

@Liz_Laugh_Luv   Maybe she wouldn't need a facial procedure. Maybe she would have become a famous scientist ⚛ travelling the world receiving prizes for breakthroughs in chemistry. We would have been so proud 🖤 of her. Which doesn't mean I'm not proud of you Pam, for who you are 💚 I am 🧡

4 hours ago   2 people like this   0 shares

@Kim_Cougar_atPlay   YIIIKES!!!! nooooo!!!! We wouldn't
want thaaaat!!!! Not for Pam!! That's terrible planning!!!!
Have you seen any of those lady scientists??? Not one of them
looks like they've ever seen the blunt end of a corrective
laser. OMG!!!! I can't even imagine what she would look like
now. She has enough problems! With her face of course. Not
her life. Well, maybe her life, just a little!! Oh GOLLEEE!!!
I can't even!!!!!

4 hours ago   2 people like this   23 shares

@Angel(a)_Face   ALRIGHT, first you take a SWIPE AT LIZ
for caring about a dog, then you SUGGEST BOY SCOUTS
and LAUGH at female scientists. Do you people have NO
BOUNDARIES?

4 hours ago   22 people like this   0 shares

@Kim_Cougar_atPlay   Ohhhh WOW!!!! Don't pay attention to
Angie! She's seeing a therapist. Now she thinks people need
boundaries!!! HA!

4 hours ago   12 people like this   0 shares

@Angel(a)_Face   Right that. BIG NEWS LADIES, it turns out
BOUNDARIES ARE A THING (thanks, therapy). Oh yeah, I
PAID for that myself too (as jaw-dropping as that is).

4 hours ago   12 people like this   0 shares

@HRHPamela   It was fun when we were all joking around,
now I'm just annoyed 😠 and disturbed 😒

4 hours ago   1 people like this   03 shares

@Angel(a)_Face   Pam finds BOUNDARIES annoying and
DISTURBING.

4 hours ago   9 people like this   0 shares

@HRHPamela   I find lack of focus annoying and disturbing 🌀 Has everyone forgotten about the funding needed here?

4 hours ago   2 people like this   3 shares

@Kim_Cougar_atPlay   Forget Pam's face lift. I've got an Amazzzzing Idea!!!! Let's use Pam's money and all go to Lizzie's monastery. Woot!!!! Girl Trip WHEEE!! Woot to Tibet!!!!

2.5 hours ago   22 people like this   3 shares

@HRHPamela   Where's my fruitcake 🍰 Did Kim eat it all?

2.5 hours ago   20 people like this   0 shares

@Angel(a)_Face   TIBET is something I can GET BEHIND.

2.5 hours ago   2 people like this   0 shares

@HRHPamela   I think you are all forgetting that not one of you has donated a penny. Please click on the KICKFUNDSTER link immediately.

2.5 hours ago   2 people like this   0 shares

@Liz_Laugh_Luv   Maybe, and this is just a suggestion 🐶 You should raise money for something you really need ❓

2.5 hours ago   2 people like this   0 shares

@Spawn_of_HRH   They're right Mom! You don't need the money for this. I think you're beautiful.

2.5 hours ago   2 people like this   0 shares

@HRHPamela By the way, everyone, I want to thank my daughter Dylane 🙄 for making this campaign happen. It was a huge job technically. I couldn't have launched it without her.

2.5 hours ago   2 people like this   0 shares

@Spawn_of_HRH   About that Mom, I need to be paid for the job soon.

2.5 hours ago   2 people like this   o shares

@HRHPamela   Right. Everyone, I hope you don't mind if I use some of the KICKFUNDSTER money to pay Dylane 🙏 Without her the KICKFUNDSTER wouldn't have launched 😇

2.5 hours ago   2 people like this   o shares

@Kim_Cougar_atPlay   OH Dylane!!!!! You are SO!!!! Talented. Would you make us a campaign for Lizzie's Sex Drive???

2.5 hours ago   2 people like this   o shares

@HRHPamela   Kim 😨 You always go too far! My daughter is NOT making you a Sex Drive.

2.5 hours ago   2 people like this   o shares

@Kim_Cougar_atPlay   OHHH KAYYY!!! So how about a Girls Getaway Drive? Tibetan monastery here we come! Celibate Monks can be kinda hot WHEW!!!

2.5 hours ago   2 people like this   o shares

@HRHPamela   First Boy Scouts 😖 Now Monks 🧕

2.5 hours ago   2 people like this   o shares

@Angel(a)_Face   I'm still ON BOARD the TIBET TRAIN.

2.5 hours ago   2 people like this   o shares

@HRHPamela   Fund my Facial first. Nobody has committed a cent yet 😒

2.5 hours ago   2 people like this   o shares

@Liz_Laugh_Luv I thought we all decided you didn't need it sweetie 💋

2.5 hours ago   2 people like this   0 shares

@HRHPamela We did not decide that! I did not 😩 All of Dylane's work will have gone for nothing 😫 And without your donations I can't pay Dylane.

2.5 hours ago   2 people like this   0 shares

@Liz_Laugh_Luv Dylane, what do you need the money for sweetheart 😻

2.5 hours ago   2 people like this   0 shares

@Spawn_of_HRH I want to take a Computer Programming course.

2.5 hours ago   2 people like this   0 shares

@Kim_Cougar_atPlay WOWEEE Dylane!!!! Personally, I would like to help with that!!! How much of our donation would you give her Pam?

2.5 hours ago   2 people like this   0 shares

@Angel(a)_Face Forget the KICKFUNDSTER, Pam. Just SEND YOUR DAUGHTER TO SCHOOL.

2.5 hours ago   2 people like this   0 shares

@HRHPamela Aw ladies 😟 If I can't afford a face lift, how can I afford to send my daughter to college?

2.5 hours ago   2 people like this   0 shares

@Angel(a)_Face Here we go...BACK to PLANNING your FUTURE. YOU should have gone to school.

2.5 hours ago   2 people like this   0 shares

@HRHPamela Well I didn't. I couldn't 😕 I was a single mom with no money.

2.5 hours ago   2 people like this   0 shares

@Angel(a)_Face Okay FULL CIRCLE. How are WE RESPONSIBLE for your youthful lack of planning?

2 hours ago   2 people like this   0 shares

@HRHPamela You're not. Of course you're not. But, maybe just to help Dylane 😗

2 hours ago   2 people like this   0 shares

@Angel(a)_Face I'm sorry, we all see how much you 🖤 your daughter. But how is your facial going to help Dylane's future?

2 hours ago   2 people like this   0 shares

@Kim_Cougar_atPlay And SWEEEET PAMMMY!!! How will it help you???

2 hours ago   2 people like this   0 shares

@HRHPamela It won't 😳 You're so right, it won't help at all.

2 hours ago   2 people like this   0 shares

@Liz_Laugh_Luv Okay 😈 we're back to cancelling the Facial KICKFUNDSTER ‼️

2 hours ago   2 people like this   0 shares

@HRHPamela Fine 😬 All of it.

2 hours ago   2 people like this   0 shares

@Angel(a)_Face   ALL of it...WHAT?

2 hours ago   2 people like this   0 shares

@HRHPamela   All of the money. 100%. All to Dylane for college. She's amazing and smart and deserving. And I'm amazing and, well, just amazing 😆

2 hours ago   2 people like this   0 shares

@Angel(a)_Face   ALRIGHT! That is ALSO something I can GET BEHIND.

2 hours ago   2 people like this   0 shares

@Liz_Laugh_Luv   You're beautiful Pam. Go look in the mirror right now. Run 🦢

2 hours ago   2 people like this   0 shares

@Spawn_of_HRH   You are Mom. Totally 👸

1 hours ago   2 people like this   0 shares

Sundowning

DEBBIE BATEMAN

IN THE UPSTAIRS ROOM of my parents' home, I stand before my father's mahogany desk. Murky light creeps in through the window. My fist holds a wad of cash.

Through the heavy silence, a voice creaks behind me. "You're nothing but a stinking thief."

Over my shoulder, I see the sagging cheeks of a sharp-eyed old woman. "It's okay, Mom. I was clearing away Dad's things. Remember, I told you we have to go through his papers."

The man hadn't said a word to me in forty years, yet he made me executor of his will. He'd been through chemo and radiation, and a final stay in a hospice, months of knowing the end was near, and he never once contacted me.

"Don't pretend I can't see what you're doing, Pauline. Where'd that money come from?"

My thumb rubs the edge of the stack. The crisp new bills snap. Like many things in my parents' lives, I don't know how to explain it. Mom never had a job other than being the wife of a judge. She'd let Dad control everything.

"Don't stand there looking stupific. I'm not a fool, you know." Mom's jaw moves like she's chewing food, her eyelids lower, and for a moment her expression freezes. "Are you stupid, girl?" She's been doing that a lot lately, messing up words and fixing them as if there's a five-second rule for dropping the wrong syllable. Change it fast enough and it's still safe to put in your mouth.

"It was at the back of his desk. Who keeps that much cash? You'd think he'd be more careful." The desk drawer is still open, and I consider tucking the money back where I found it. If I move fast enough, maybe she'll forget what she saw. I can go back later when she's not watching and retrieve it without causing a fuss.

Dusk is the hardest time of day. The fading light worsens the confusion, makes her do things she'd never have done before. She's forgotten to do up all the buttons on her mauve silk shirt. Peekaboo glimpses of skin and a faded bra show through the gaps.

"Don't play innocent with me, missy. You've been going through my stuff and taking things. First you tricked me into letting you into the office. Now you're stealing from me."

I pinch my lips and shake my head. "For crying out loud, Mom, stop this nonsense. Listen to what you're saying."

A boney finger jabs at my face. "I'm going to call the police. I'm going to have you arrested."

I slap the wad of cash into her hand. "Fine then, take it."

Her face blanches, the cheeks slackening, her mouth hanging open. I'm telling myself she's out of reach, when all at once her faraway mind awakens, bright eyed and fully on, all of her attention focussed on me.

I can't stop myself. In the hidden places of my mind, a secret thrill rises.

| Over the years, I'd tried to stay in contact with Mom. We'd have secret meetings in parks and restaurants, quiet late-night phone calls. When even those stopped, I'd figured she'd

done what she always did to me—back away and turn silent. If I'd been in closer touch, I'd have known she was having problems.

I'm face to face with it now and my daughter has been dragged along with me. I never asked her to interrupt her studies, but when Emma sees a problem she can't help wanting to fix it. It's her best quality and her worst. She's doing a master's in social work. Her thesis is on Alzheimer's, and she claims this is an opportunity for research.

I can't deny she brings an air of calm to the impossible situation. After the incident with the cash, there's nothing I can do to settle Mom down. Then Emma returns, and within minutes, she has Mom resting easy in her favourite winged-back chair in front of a nature show on TV.

Eager to finish, I return to Dad's office. The sooner I settle the accounts, the sooner we can decide what to do about Mom, and Emma can return to her studies. I'm old enough to get a senior's discount some places. It's time we all forgot what happened to me as a child. No matter how long I stand at attention at his desk, Dad will never come up behind me. But the feeling is the same, gasping for breath, holding it at the back of my nose like a warning, tiny shivers at the sides of my face, tingles along my lips, the scent of wet leather.

Most kids were spanked in their own room on their own bed. I took my punishment on my feet, in my father's office, bent over his antique mahogany desk. The desk with swirly grain like crushed fur and cup-style pull-handles made of brass.

Mom would disappear behind a closed door somewhere in our Elbow Park house to fold warm sheets in the laundry, read a paperback in the library, sort the canned goods in our pantry. Who knows what she was doing? She kept her small-mouthed face hidden until hours later when she crept into my room wearing a velvet housecoat and downcast eyes.

Perched on the edge my bed, she'd sing "Fly Me to the Moon," as if it were a secret only the two of us shared, the bright notes barely contained within a whisper. I sometimes forgot she'd been a professional singer before she got married. A normal mother and child might have cuddled. Yet, for most of the song, she looked away. Only for the last three words would she turn her attention on me. She'd whisper-sing, I love you, and her lips would brush my hair, the only physical contact she made.

After she left, the scent of her perfume remained, lily of the valley with a trail of jasmine. The perfume was fresh, clear, and blindingly false. She'd never mention what he did. She'd never say it was wrong, she'd never try to stop him, and I pretended not to notice how my own mother preferred not to touch me.

There should be more than enough money to put her into a home. According to the websites, she could have a private studio with mountain views, stimulating programs, a spa, a beauty salon, a fitness centre, attentive staff. They call the services they provide "memory care." But what does she remember—sorting the pantry, reading a book, doing laundry?

I empty the last of Dad's desk into the trash. The important papers are safely stored in a box. Mom probably has the wad of cash I slapped into her hand stuffed into one of her pockets. By morning, she'll have forgotten it's there.

| When I stop by the kitchen to say goodbye to Emma, Mom is still watching a nature show.

"I think I'll be going," I say, buttoning my jacket.

Emma turns from the stove. "Okay, Mom. I can handle it from here."

She ought to be at home making her own dinner, or hanging out with friends, not here in this big lonely house with an old woman who accuses people of things they'd never do. My hands find the car keys at the bottom of my purse.

"Wait a minute," she says. "One more thing." Emma goes to the kitchen table where Mom's sweater hangs over a chair. She reaches into the pockets and gathers the cash, which she brings to me. "Quick. Take this away."

I stuff the money into my purse. The TV continues to blare from the adjoining room, but Mom must have been listening to us all along. She marches into the room with her chin jutting out. "What do you have in that purse, Pauline?"

Before I can escape, Mom rips the purse off my shoulder. My belongings empty onto the floor and she snatches the cash. A frothy bubble of whitish spittle hangs on her bottom lip. "This doesn't beebong to you." With a shake of her head, she erases her words and tries again. "It's not yours. Don't take things that aren't yours!"

Emma walks up to my mom, their eyes meet, and together they form a cocoon of mutual attention that shuts everyone else out. At university, she took a course that teaches an approach called Validation. According to Emma, it's the best way to help people with Alzheimer's.

"You think this money was stolen?"

"I know it."

"The money is important to you."

"All my life people have been taking things from me. I only want what's mine. Is that too much to ask?"

"No, it isn't."

Mom's frown melts away and her liver-coloured mouth curls into a smile. "Thank you, my sweet girl."

Emma returns to the stove and Mom follows without resistance. Her weight shifts from one foot to the other, but she remains glued to Emma's side. Neither of them notices me leaving.

| When I was a child, Mom was always in the kitchen, traipsing from stove to sink to counter, making pot roast, lasagna, or my favourite, shepherd's pie. Steam lifted off the potatoes mashed with butter and cream. Mom fried the hamburger with onions, a splash of dry red wine, baby peas, and carrots cut into tiny cubes. She coated the top with sharp cheddar that browned extra dark in the oven.

I'd follow the swish of her cotton, the slink of her satin. She wore dresses too fancy for any homemaker. One day, a pink cotton swing dress. Another day, an emerald pencil dress with a waterfall peplum across the front. The dresses remained hidden under a pinafore apron most of the time. Her aprons were every bit as impressive as the dresses. Pink with white polka dots, navy blue with daisy accents, ruffled pockets and floppy strings that tied into extravagant bows.

Children will believe in all sorts of nonsense—Santa, gnomes, fairies. A skinny thing in white leotards and plaid shift dresses, I wasn't any different. I believed a single look from Mom was all I needed to withstand the heavy brow of Dad's disapproval, the bite of his words, the humiliation of his office desk and what so often came after.

I'd pause when she paused, both of us lined up at the stove. I'd stand on one foot hoping to be noticed as if it was a magic spell, and if only I kept my balance, if only I didn't wobble, Mom would turn. Her green eyes would awaken, the freckles on her cheeks would rise, and the corners of her mouth would curl, all for me, her little girl.

| A week passes while Emma and I debate what to do with Mom. Emma is entertaining the notion of taking care of her

for several months or even a year. She's encouraged by a few small moments of calm. Then something bad happens, as I knew it would.

"Is your mother Helen Shaw?"

At the sound of her name, I press the phone closer. I'm at work when I find out. "Yes."

"There's been a bit of an upset with your mom," the man says slowly.

Ever since I came back into contact with Mom, I've been waiting for it to happen. I expected a call from the police, or worse, the hospital. I never expected the call to come from a financial institution and a guy who says he's a client care representative.

"We have her in a quiet room now," he says. "But she needs a ride home. She was having a few challenges with the bank machine. When staff tried to help, she became flustered." He clears his throat, lowers his voice. "We had to intervene."

By the time I arrive, Mom's as demure as I remember her being on our trips through the city to see the dentist or doctor when I was a child. Such occasions called for a mink coat and sunglasses. Mom has neither fashion item now, only a beige trench coat and reading glasses perched too far down her nose.

They've given her a cup of tea and a biscuit. She's nibbling and sipping like a lady. Who would guess moments earlier she'd been a whirl of sharp fingernails at the ends of flaying arms? More than a bit of an upset, I would say. She'd scratched a teller in the face, drawing blood. She'd had to be held back or she might've done worse.

Later, I examine the bank statements. I'd been so busy tidying up Dad's bills and gathering his investments, I hadn't looked closely at their joint account. It started when he went into hospice. Every few days, someone took out cash, sometimes hundreds of dollars. But the incident with the teller seems to be the only time she tried to take out money after Emma moved in.

| When we return, Emma is in the foyer waiting. She eases Mom out of her trench coat and guides her into the house. In the kitchen, she points to a glass of milk on the countertop. "Have a rest. If you like, take your milk and settle yourself in the dining room. Supper will be ready soon."

Mom staggers to the dining room, slopping milk and settling into a chair exactly as Emma asked her to.

Emma rejoins me in the kitchen. "What did they do to poor Grandma?" she whispers.

"Poor Grandma? You can't be serious. Your poor Grandma attacked a clerk at the bank. We're lucky they didn't press charges. She left scratch marks on the man's face."

"I should've kept her nails shorter. I shouldn't have let her go out alone. She said she was only walking around the block. She's done that lots of times without anything happening. I thought the fresh air would be good for her."

"Honey, it's nothing you did. It's nothing any of us have done, although we're paying for it. You should be in school, and I can't keep missing work."

Emma wipes her eyes and refastens her ponytail tighter than before. "Leave if you have to. I'll handle things here."

If I don't do something, my daughter will keep throwing herself into the same unforgiving situation. The sun will go down and none of us can stop it. The illness will only get worse.

"It's time we put her into care. We can't put it off a day longer. That's final."

| They give Mom a room of her own, a studio apartment, really, with a bedroom and sitting area, and a kitchenette that is only for making tea because it doesn't have a stove. They come once a week and clean her bathroom and the rest of the place. Three times a day, they serve delicious gourmet meals.

It's surprisingly easy to move her. Emma made such a fuss I had to trick her, but Mom never puts up the least bit of resistance, at least not when I take her out of the house. I wait in my car until the lights go out in Emma's room. I let myself in through the front door and creep through the house.

I find Mom in bed in her dimly lit room. She's patting the pillow in the empty space beside her and she's humming "Fly Me to the Moon." In a blinding moment of hope, I think of kissing her wrinkly forehead and telling her to go to sleep.

Recently, she's been getting more and more confused. Maybe that's why she does what I say when I lean towards her and suggest it'd be best if she gets dressed. My parents always had season's tickets to the symphony. I tell her we're going to an evening of Gershwin. In the past, she'd have worn a simple black dress with pearls, but she chooses orange pants and a pink shirt. And by the time we've driven across town and arrived at the manor, she's forgotten where we're going.

The staff are pleased to accommodate our late arrival. Mom doesn't know why we're there. The place looks more like a five-star hotel than an advanced-care residence. The lobby is filled with winged-back chairs and elegant maple side tables. The wide hallways have thick carpet, and the walls are adorned with original art.

A personal care worker is standing by, even though it's two o'clock in the morning. My parents' money pays for a lot of services. The personal care worker has a bad perm and a mouth that means business. "Take it easy, Helen," she says, guiding Mom by the arm down the hall. I follow behind, feeling useless. Mom is better off in someone else's hands. Once inside the suite, the care worker deposits her into a brand-new lift chair. "Now, isn't that better? Rest a bit. We'll have you settled into a nice warm bed soon."

It's probably the lift chair that sets Mom off. Back home she sat in the same chair she'd always used. The minute her back presses the lift chair, her leg strikes out, her sharp-toed shoe stabbing the caregiver's crotch.

"You are not my girl. Where's my sweet girl? What have you done to her?"

| By the next day, Emma is settled into the manor in the tiny suite meant for one. We agree that she'll stay with Mom a week or two, but after that she's going back to her studies. Now that the hardest choice has been made, she seems willing to be reasonable.

But two months later, Emma is still there. I visit as much as I can. I know I should show up more often. Twilight has darkened the present moment, insisting on its forward momentum into oblivion, trapping us all in a confusion of light that is neither bright nor dark.

When I step into her suite, Mom is stationed in her lift chair, a green plaid afghan over her lap. A glass of water rests on the overbed table at her side. Her face is slack, her mouth sloppy, and her eyes gaze into nothing. Since moving into the place where they're supposed to give her memory extra care, she's deteriorated rapidly.

I set the shoebox on the small table in her kitchenette. We can talk about the contents later when the time seems right. We've all learned to assess Mom's condition before introducing something new into her world. I'd used the shoebox to collect the money hidden throughout their house. I didn't feel safe carrying all that cash, but I wanted to see her face when she saw what I'd found—nearly eight thousand dollars.

I sit on a hard, wooden chair beside Mom. Emma watches from across the room. Mom takes long breaths, in and out through her nose, a faint wheeze followed by a louder huff. I touch the back of her hand, feel the bluntness of her knuckles and the loose dry skin. When she shows no sign of having been touched, I increase the pressure a little, one squeeze with a quick release. Mom flinches, her hand slipping out from mine and disappearing under the blanket.

"Who let this woman into my room?" Thin white hair flings across her face, a strand sticking to the corner of her eye. "Get her away from me."

All my life Mom has been an absence, her body an empty space, evidence only of what is not there. Wherever she goes, she leaves behind a vacuum. I do what I can to stay out of the vortex, keep a safe distance, protect myself. But even now, when I am well into my fifties, no longer a girl, and Mom is old and fragile of body and mind, I still get sucked into the abyss.

I cannot escape her words. They echo in the hollow of my mind, a final answer to the dread I've carried in my stomach for as long as I can remember. All the years of hoping for a flash of her attention, wanting only a minute and hating that want, wishing instead to be free and not care. And now none of it matters.

| After Mom doesn't recognize me, I don't visit for a week. I speak every night to Emma on the phone to make sure everything's okay. That's what draws me back. Emma has tried to take the money to the bank, but every time she touches the shoebox, Mom starts thrashing her arms. She's

taken to keeping the shoebox beside her in bed at night and carrying it around like a baby in her arms during the day.

I suggest we grab the shoebox when Mom is napping. Given her memory, it shouldn't be too hard to remove the source of upset. All we have to do is take it away. If she doesn't see it, she won't remember it exists. That's how short her memory has become.

She's snoring when we creep into her bedroom. Emma holds back the covers. I lean over the bed, reaching for the shoebox.

Mom's eyes snap open. She clutches the shoebox to her chest and steps out of the bed. Her confused gaze goes straight to Emma. "Pauline!" she says in a crackly voice. "Keep that person away from me."

I'm not surprised to hear my daughter called that name. Emma warned me it'd been happening. And yet, I wonder how Mom really feels, what she'd do if given the chance to change her life, what this dream she's concocted in the mixed-up synapses of her clogged-up brain means to the real world here and now.

Mom slips into her pink bathrobe and saunters out of the room with the shoebox under her arm. She's found a new kind of grace since losing more memory. Her movements have grown languid, without restraint. She could be sleep-walking. Once seated at the dining table, she unpacks the box and starts counting, muttering words that do not quite make sense. "One. Tooter. Three. Four. Five. Sexty."

"Let me take care of this," says Emma.

Mom's eyes keep darting to the side as if she's expecting someone, as if she's afraid. Her coordination is not what it used to be. She can only drop one stack of bills into the shoebox at a time. "Quick, help me!" she whispers.

Emma joins in. Soon all the money is stashed away and the lid is back on. Mom looks from side to side, making sure the coast is clear. Her scrawny arms reach across the table and drag the shoebox closer. She tries to tuck it under her bathrobe, but it's too big and looks ridiculous. Half the box isn't covered.

Her grey head sinks into her shoulders. "Pauline," she hisses. "Don't you ever let him open that lid. Never. Ever. Never. No matter what happens, never let him see what's inside."

An unprepared person would shake their head at the absurdity of the situation, but Emma knows what to do. In a panicky whisper, mirroring the old woman's, Emma reassures her that she is there, and they are sharing whatever moment is happening.

"You don't want him to see what's in the box?"

Mom nods.

Emma leans closer. "What would happen if he looked inside?"

With a huff, Mom blurts out her answer. "He would see what I have...and he would take it." Her wrinkly hand reaches out and snatches the air. "All my life, he's been taking things from me. I've told you that before."

Emma nods. "What did he take?"

She pinches her mouth and the room fills with silence. The familiar absence threatens to darken us all. Only this time is different. Something new happens, something I've never seen before.

Mom looks upward. The line of her jaw grows strong. Pain washes over her face, and she widens her mouth in a show of teeth, yellow and worn but still strong. "My sweet little girl. She was my whole life and he took her from me. I hate him."

| Mom still cradles the shoebox in her arms and sleeps with it at night, but we've replaced the bundles of cash with photocopies of dollar bills. Before returning full-time to her studies, Emma picked out a caregiver. It's worked out well. I visit as often as I can.

Two days before Christmas, we book a private dining room at the manor. While staff members serve turkey dinner, we sit at the massive table with silver utensils on a white tablecloth.

My daughter has finished her thesis. Graduation is in the spring. As we eat our salad, she talks about her new position at the hospital. I toast my daughter. The three of us raise our glasses, and as happens sometimes these days, Mom spills a little on her chin.

Emma is the first to push back her chair, but I hold out my hand. As the room fills with silence, I wait for my daughter's sky-blue eyes to find my face. "I'll take care of this," I say.

With a crisp white napkin, I wipe Mom's chin, and we continue our meal.

Perfect Purple Rose

ELIZABETH GREENE

i

Sharon Olds says, *Poets have no age.*
She was in her sixties when I took her workshop.
She could have been forty—or twenty.
Wise, dedicated, but playful as a girl,
with sea-grey eyes, hair smooth as driftwood,
sea and sand, rhythm of waves.
When she smiled, waves sparkled,
sand glowed gold.
Fifteen years later, photos show
her cheekbones even more sculpted,
her eyes unswerving.

Her poetry, ageless.

In the centre of the workshop table,
a perfect purple rose,
longing to be a poem.

ii

I am not Sharon Olds,
don't have her great poetic gifts,
her soul's straight spine,
though I've spent a lifetime
chasing words, *veritatem dilexi*,
I have loved the truth.
Words cut through time,
don't depend on crumbling plaster
or cracking canvas,
don't need to be breathed
into life again
like music.
Poems exist outside time
though reading and writing
both depend on breath and blood,
the heartbeat's measure.

In any case, the world
they come from, the world
of the imagination
has no age.

Maybe it's a lifetime spent
with one foot in that other world.
But maybe it's that people
tend to get me wrong.
In my mid-teens,
I looked nineteen or twenty.
When I started teaching,
I'd come to class
the first day of each school year,
lurk at the side of the room.

No one guessed I was the professor
until I claimed my space,
began the class.
Even in my fifties,
I was still declining
student discounts.
Or maybe it's my age-of-innocence
grandmother, so that I stayed unknowing
till now, in my seventies,
I may not look my age, but
I'm starting to
look like
who I am.

iii
My Great Aunt Rose, frail,
in a good black dress,
cane beside her chair,
receives birthday wishes.
All I see is white hair, thin arms,
a memorable face, which I can't fathom,
a woman on the shore of the River of Life,
in the country of old age.

All I remember is the window facing west
over the Hudson, the river grey with ice,
sinking sun yellow through grey clouds,
and delectable cookies, inexhaustible,
family members I'd scarcely met
and didn't remember.
(Why didn't my mother, whose perceptions
I relied on then, translate for me, tell me
who all these people were?)

What my great aunt must have seen:
the teenage granddaughter of her late sister,
the same dark hair, the family mouth,
dark, unreadable eyes.

Appearances are deceiving.
Aunt Rose lived another dozen years.
She left me my grandmother's dining-room buffet.
You don't want it, do you? asked my mother.
I do, I said. It was splendid.
Dark fruitwood, with a flowing grain.
All the curves and curls you'd ever want,
Inlaid panels with upward-reaching wheat and roses.
Refinished, it's graced my parties for fifty years.
My house is small, but the buffet still glows welcome,
as it did for my great-grandmother, my grandmother
and my Great Aunt Rose.

BODY

you will be amazed

LAURIE MACFAYDEN

you won't believe! these incredible websites
that will take years! off your saggy wrinkly
middle-aged face and ease you into dotage

for women:
compliments over 40 dotcom
compliments over 50 dotcom
areas that sag over 60 dotcom
get younger skin right away dotcom
skin-tightening masks dotcom
fake fuller lips dotcom
embrace grey brows dotcom
look 10 years younger in 10 days dotcom
how can i look hot at 50 dotcom
how can i look hot at 70 dotcom
keep your pucker primed dotcom
say goodbye to skin blotches dotcom
don't throw away the end of the cucumber dotcom

make a paste of (choose any three) crushed rock salt,
turmeric, honey, coffee, chocolate, red wine, avocado,
buttermilk, oatmeal, egg white, milk.
apply to face for 15 or 45 minutes.
scrape off and say hello to a younger you!

pro tip: *can also be refrigerated up to five days and served as*
party dip

for men:
how to text older women you like dotcom
compliments women can't resist dotcom
compliments women desperately want but men never
    give dotcom
you will be amazed how fast insecure vulnerable wrinkly
rich old women will fall for your compliments dotcom

embrace your natural hair colour (fact: women find grey
    hair sexy!)
use under-eye cream every day

pro tip: *get your body hair under control*

Mastery of the Instrument

JOANN MCCAIG

THE YEAR before I turned sixty, I scared the crap out of myself. I was visiting my friend Janine in Spain, and I glimpsed the future. My future. I saw frailty, I saw vulnerability, and I saw it coming for me.

My bus got in from Nerja at noon. Janine met me there and guided me down a boardwalk to the marina neighbourhood of Malaga. Her little apartment seemed a paradise, a miracle—sundrenched white stucco, the endless Mediterranean vista. And inside, colourful furniture and tablecloths and flowers. "Like something out of a dream," I told her, this vibrant woman of sixty-five who has taken a year's leave from her ESL job at a university to teach in Spain.

Janine looks young for her age, glows with health and happiness, shows off her trim arms and body in a black tank top and skinny jeans (yet another of my friends who wears skinny jeans tucked into knee high boots, a look I probably have the body for, but not the nerve). On the dresser in the small bedroom of her suite is a photo of her cuddling with a man. Her friend. The friend she was just travelling with. In the Rif mountains of Morocco.

Janine said, "I need to use the loo," and while she was in there, quite a long time actually, I took a look around. Noticed a piece of paper on the kitchen table. It looked like a list of things to do. My eye fell on "11:40 get dressed." And I averted my eyes, embarrassed. For Janine.

We spent that day together in Malaga. A seaside restaurant, her easy conversation with a man selling loaves of bread from a big basket. The Picasso museum. Her pissing me off as we walked through some Roman ruins, an ancient amphitheatre and soaring brick walls of a Moorish fortress. Some know-it-all remark she made. I suppose that the two of us could have spent that evening together in those lively Malaga streets, the broad shining city squares bustling with life. But truth to tell, Janine sometimes makes me tired.

So I got on an early bus back to Nerja. Janine stood on the sidewalk at the depot waving goodbye for an excessively long time. And on the bus, a man sat next to me and chatted me up. In French. He spoke to me in French for the entire one hour and fifteen minutes of the trip, and when we got off the bus, he invited me out for a coffee or a drink. I said *non merci, je suis fatiguée.*

Trying to talk to him, trying to follow in my halting French just made me tired. Besides, I knew that he was not really interested in me at all, he just wanted somebody to talk at.

My mind kept drifting back to that list on Janine's table. 11:10 yoga, 11:30 eat, 11:40 get dressed. This brave pathetic old woman who dresses and acts like a girl, the biking, the adventures, the new lover, the dopesmoking in Morocco. All blown to smithereens by an abject scared little note on the table. 11:10 yoga, 11:30 eat, 11:40 get dressed. There were about six items on the list, meeting me at the bus stop probably the last one. But I had only glanced at it then looked

away, embarrassed at the sudden naked vulnerability of an
old woman, of my friend Janine.

But since then, I've learned a few things

When I was a child I studied piano, the Royal Conservatory
program. On the title page of my music book were the words
"leading to mastery of the instrument." I did not master the
piano. In fact, my teacher suggested to my mother, after a
couple of years of lessons, "perhaps JoAnn would do better
in a dance class?"

So, no, I did not master the piano, but in my sixties, I have
in fact achieved mastery of my own instrument in several key
areas. Such as...

Backside

The proper name is *proctalgia fugax* (a fleeting pain in the
ass) and it's the result of multiple pregnancies, especially the
last baby, who weighed in at 8 pounds 13, can you imagine?
Head like a cantaloupe!

Here's how it works now that you've mastered it: you
wake in the middle of the night. A persistent not ache but
active pain, yes, in the rectum. The 'rhoids, the piles. Pain
like a red-hot poker. You know that you will not be able to
fall back to sleep. So you implement your pain in the ass
routine. Run hot bath water three inches deep. Swallow some
analgesic—Tylenol, aspirin, whatever's on hand—grab ice
pack from freezer, cover in a clean rag and roll back into bed,
awkwardly squeezing the ice pack between the cheeks and
holding it there for as long as you can manage. Then, hoisting
nightie up around shoulders (too cold to be naked), go sit in
the steaming sitz bath, in water as hot as you can stand. Sit
there until bored and sleepy. Last step? Dab the offending

area with the prescription cream. Yes, there have been occasions when you have become complacent in your mastery
and have stopped carrying the necessary ointment tube with
you. Remember begging that dour Scottish pharmacist?
Remember attempting to mime the problem at a *pharmacia* in
Mexico? But now, you're the Butt Queen (apologies to Louise
Erdrich), and within an hour, you are back to sleep.

It's good to be older and not terrified of your frailties
anymore. You are learning how to live in this decaying body
and are no longer offended by its betrayals. Time was when
proctalgia fugax would strike and leave you gasping and help-
less—remember how you likened it to your ex-husband,
that other fleeting pain in the ass? Remember that time
on the way to hockey with the kids, how scared they were
when you had to pull over and sit hunched over the steering
wheel, gasping with pain? Remember that time on a deserted
highway in Saskatchewan? You stopped at a gas station,
bought a chilled can of pop, drove on a mile then stopped,
unzipped your jeans and tucked the can into the zone, sitting
on it for ten minutes, tears streaming, wondering how you
were ever going to get home.

So yes, in your dotage, it may be true that you sometimes
need help from a non-senior with file management on your
laptop...

But pile management? Sister, you've got it *down*.

Skin

And then there are your Old Woman Hands. Which for some
reason are highly vulnerable to slivers. Not sure why. Thin
skin? Dryness?

You have learned not to handle firewood at all unless you
are wearing work gloves. Then, one time, you noticed teeny
slivers appearing at the same place on your fingers, two odd

places: the inside of the ring finger, the knuckle of the index. Examined your work gloves and found a couple of small holes that had let the slivers in. The persistence of those little slivers in finding their way through your gloves is a matter for cosmic speculation best saved for another day. So you just throw out the holey gloves, thankful that they come in six packs.

But then yesterday, you got a sliver from the wooden match you used to light the fire! In the crease of the third finger of your right hand, in the midst of a major writing day! The forest is clearly out for revenge! Perhaps it's all those trees that have given their lives in support of your writing ambitions?

You poured on lots of peroxide and tugged at the sliver, but no luck.

Then in the night, you awoke. (Is this becoming a theme?)

No butt crisis this time, just waking in the night, and for this you have also developed a calming routine, a strategy. You make a piece of toast and eat it. You brew a cup of decaf black tea with milk and take it back to bed and drink it while reading until your eyes feel heavy. (Not being afraid of insomnia anymore is another useful milestone, no kidding.)

When you wake these nights, you feel cobwebby around the eyes, and indeed you can see spiders on the ceiling of your room when you put your glasses on.

Anyhow, this one night, the sliver night, you eat your toast and even though you can hardly see from the spidery webs, go into the bathroom and seek the sliver with the only pair of tweezers in the house. And you get it! You snag that pesky sliver on the first try.

The victory feels so sweet!

A moment of good luck for Old Woman Hands in the middle of the night! Hurrah!

Pleasure

What a young thing can't appreciate is the joy of knowing this old body inside and out. Of developing an autoerotic routine that delivers reliable results efficiently and pleasantly every time.

Remember that day when you were working on a story that had a lot of sexual energy and found it odd that you didn't feel very turned on, though the utter and complete absence of estrogen might have had something to do with it? In fact, a while back you'd confessed to a friend "these days, I have to put self-pleasure on my to-do list!"

But then you sent the story off to your editor and over a celebratory cup of herbal tea (the champagne and caviar of your age group) you thought, it's been a while, why not give myself a little?

So you prepared the few items you need. And the music? Well there are a couple of rock tunes you used to favour, but Bach is on the stereo at the moment and you can't be bothered to change it so—

You begin. And oh my god you're only a minute or two into a process that usually takes at least ten minutes, and oh my god do you ever go off, awash, a-shudder, fireworks, and then collapsing on the bed, laughing.

"Holy crap, I guess it has been a while," you think, still laughing.

That upstart boy Hamlet said to his mother, "At your age, the heyday in the blood is tame. It's humble, and waits upon judgement."

What the hell does Hamlet know?

Contentment

So there's mastery, good luck, pleasant surprises. And then there's plain old contentment. And truly, there's much contentment in the rhythm of old woman days and nights.

You sleep in late, your old dog and you. All those years up at 7, 6:30, one year 6:15 when the school bus came super early.

Then you'd hit the floor running, lunches in bags, homework in knapsacks, socks, shoes. Wave goodbye then get yourself off to work. Saturday mornings were such a luxury, if no early hockey.

Now old woman and old dog sleep in late, most days. 8, 8:30, sometimes even 9. Coffee in bed, two cups, and iPad scrabble for the human. A few more dreams and light farts for the dog.

Time to get up. You both stretch, human all the way up and all the way down, twice. Canine upward dog then downward.

Your day begins.

Kibble with omega oil and fish treat.

Orange and banana cut up on a plate, with gluten-free granola and unsweetened hemp milk.

And in the evening, canine dinner promptly at 5. You resist early dining, which to your way of thinking is a sign of irreparable senility. You remember moving your mother into The Home and how Mom steadfastly refused to "go down" before 6, sneering at those lost souls gathered outside the dining room doors at 4:30. Then Mom gradually relented to 5:30, then 5. Passed away before the bar dropped any further.

This old woman—you, her daughter—holds off until 6:30, or tries to. And after dinner, in the evening, when you put Bill Evans live at the Village Vanguard on the stereo, the old dog lifts her head from the couch at the sound of the background noise in the jazz club and barks at the intruders. Every single time. And every single time, she makes you smile.

Bedtime? Well, the old dog sleeps on the couch most of the day and has to be woken up to be told it's time to go to bed. You strive to stay out of the bedroom until 9, make an effort to keep the bedroom light on until at least 10. Point of miniscule pride.

Your dreams are exhausting: mad adventures, pulse-pounding dilemmas, heroic·challenges, travel, romance, drama, melodrama. You awake refreshed and rested, and after two cups of coffee and a game of iPad scrabble, you stretch with the dog and begin your day.

Discontent

One thing you really hate is how old men think they can stick it to you by flirting with young women in your presence. And you can't really blame the young women for going along with it. It's their due, after all. (In fact, that's what made such easy pickings for a creep like Ted Bundy. The young women he approached didn't want to seem ungrateful for the attention.)

Like that old weasel G at the bookstore event the other night. You have politely ignored the way he twirls his glass at you, wanting more wine, because you have your instructions from the store manager, one fill per customer. G's conversation is not dull though, the man is at least well read and okay there is a moment when you wonder if he is single, but then as he turns to leave, he says to the twenty-two-year-old staff member standing beside you "and what is your name again?" as if she would ever give a veiny-nosed coot like him the time of day anyhow.

Too bad G's gone by the time you're saying goodbye to the staff at the front door, so he doesn't hear that nice young man Paul inviting you to go for a drink with them all. Paul's with his beautiful stilettoed girlfriend, but he always makes a point of flirting politely with you, a young man properly brought up, probably by a woman not unlike yourself. And you say *oh, no thanks, I need to go home.* And this handsome young guy smiles and says I wish I could do that, too. Pause. *I mean to my home, not yours—because it would be weird if I went to your home.*

You both laugh at this, but of course you are too tired (and, okay, too old) to think to say *Well it would sure confuse the dog!* At least until he and the other young folk are out the door.

A funny thing though, try this as an experiment. Approach a newly acquainted young man and young woman talking at a social event. More often than not, the guy will be polite, but the young woman will freeze you out like a glacier. Why, you wonder, when really what you could do is make her look really good. But you realize that she does not want to look at you because in you she sees her future—cross-hatched cheeks, the effects of gravity on chin, breasts and butt—and it is a future that scares the living shit out of her.

Just wait, my young friend. Just you wait 'til it becomes second nature to grab your crotch every time you feel a sneeze coming on. And who doesn't remember that rite of passage, the first time you jump on a trampoline after having given birth? The shock of urine trickling down the leg?

And yet...

These small indignities, these little leaks, are nothing, compared to the rights and freedoms of cronehood. Such as:

1. The absolute inalienable right to be cranky, and especially to object loudly and frequently to the general dumbing down and mindless crudity of much of contemporary culture. (Have you ever listened to "I Love It" by Kanye West? Tried to

watch a network sitcom? This is the freedom of expression we fought for?)

2. To take no interest at all in certain aspects of contemporary culture. (I decided to *just not care* about *Sex and the City*. At all. Ever. And my quality of life has not been adversely affected in the least.)

3. To leave at intermission if not interested in what happens next.

4. To set aside a book after ten pages, ditto.

5. To stop on the sidewalk to converse with robins and squirrels.

6. To rest in the middle of the day, if tired. (And oh yes, very important, the unassailable right to be tired. To say *non, merci, je suis fatiguée*.)

7. To do things more slowly. I've noticed how my son reacts with dismay when he watches me negotiate with a WestJet check-in machine at a pace that suits me perfectly, but signals to him that I am seriously in decline. He sees in me what I saw in Janine seven years ago.

How abjectly I feared the vulnerability I saw in Janine's list of things to do on that morning I visited her in Malaga. But I know now that Janine was just keeping herself organized, and that my own fears about what that list meant were groundless. I will age, I will slow down, I will make lists—okay, I don't yet have to remind myself to get dressed, but perhaps that's on the horizon. I have been blessed, so far, with no serious infirmity, no health catastrophe—though when that comes, I expect I will somehow find ways to cope.

My enemy is not aging at all; it's the fear of it. And certainly, there are plenty of things to be legitimately fearful about these days—my children's future, the health of the planet, and the collapse of democracy come most immediately to mind—but fear of aging?

Nah.

Conclusion: A secret joy

William Blake's odd little poem "The Sick Rose" talks of a dark secret love that destroys a bed of crimson joy. His words swim in my head and rearrange as I try to find a way to describe a phenomenon that has probably always been with me, in this body, but which I've only in the last decade slowed down enough, calmed down enough, to notice. It's the secret joy of touching a patch of my flesh—near the corner of my mouth, the curve of a hip, the soft rolls below the navel, the ankle bone—and feeling a rush of sensation, of liveliness and delight that simply suffuses my entire being.

Rest assured that this joy is general, not genital, and the beauty of it is that it comes only unbidden, as a gift, a surprise. It cannot be courted or sought. It just arrives. I'm reading, or in bed trying to sleep, or on the couch watching either *Downton Abbey* or a football game, and my finger grazes a patch of my skin. And finds an exquisite tingle of lively pleasure there. Profound, richly satisfying, stop-me-in-my-tracks wonder. Mortal flesh that is utterly awake.

My own flesh, reminding me: *Be joyful. You are alive. You are still alive.*

Body Composition

WENDY MCGRATH

These bodies of ours are, after all, the homes of our souls.
—RUTH DRAPER, "A Class in Greek Poise"

I. My avatar

When I get a new phone, I create an avatar. One of those
funny little characters that look like you but, of course, are
not really you. I play Dr. Frankenstein as I choose my avatar's
body parts. From these inanimate body parts my avatar will
animate my texts, add a bit of humour, a bit of whimsy, and a
touch of emoticon. Eyes: blue. Face: round. Body type: meso-
morph. Mouth: Cupid's bow, red. Clothes: sneakers, jeans,
T-shirt, long jacket. Glasses: large black-rimmed Ray-Bans
I wear to see my way into the distance. Nose: father's side.
Ears: ones I like. Hair colour: grey. I stopped dyeing my hair.
Grey is my real hair colour now. It's an *un*covery.

My avatar does look like me, though. I've been honest—
I haven't made myself taller or thinner. The avatar will embody
an endless choice of greetings, emotions, and situations.
Good morning. I need coffee. Sad. Angry. Going to the gym.
Eating. Drinking. Waiting. Whatever.

My avatar and its reactions in its phone life have become an inside joke between me and my family and friends. One little image can represent the comedy and tragedy in a moment. But it will never allow a look inside the actual body and, if there is such a thing, the soul. My avatar is really bodiless and soulless. I've been honest in my avatar's representation of me, but my avatar still cannot be true. There's nothing going wrong beneath the cartoon-caricature surface of its exterior. There is no pain in the body parts I've chosen, no weakening of the eyesight or the bones.

II. Body composition

At various times in my life I've directed my focus on various parts of my body. Breasts. Legs. Nose. Now, having rounded the curve past middle age, it was what couldn't be seen by the naked eye that had motivated me to go for a fitness assessment at the gym.

I'd always imagined every bone in my body coursing with calcium. Strong. My very bones fed by sunbeams, transforming cheese and yogurt I ate into vitamin D with invisible wonder. The only thing I'd ever broken was a toe—no big deal. I am also what you'd classify as "very active." I go to a gym where I do spin, weight, cardio, and yoga classes. I walk along the North Saskatchewan River and ride my bike. I considered myself unbreakable.

So, when I had a bone density test and my doctor told me the ghostly blurs she pointed to signified osteopenia in my back and osteoporosis in my hips, I was gobsmacked. When did this change in my body composition occur? When did my bones, when did I, become breakable?

My doctor gave me a list of things to do to deal with osteoporosis, or "Oz" as I nicknamed it. The list included a once-a-week pill, a daily calcium tablet, drinking only three cups of coffee or tea a day, one alcoholic drink a day, and thirty minutes of weight-bearing exercise daily. Knowing what's happening inside my body, I decide to get a fitness assessment with a trainer at the gym, sharpen my focus.

III. Here I am

I generally don't spend time in the large main gym area with the machines, the music—which gives the gym more dance-floor than gym-floor feel—the TV screens—which always seem to be on the food channel. For the most part, I stick to the exercise classes in the mirrored room upstairs or in the spin room. On this particular morning I wait in front of a sign titled "Floor Etiquette" posted on the gym wall. Like some shining sacred tablet, it is engraved with gym command-ments: *Proper attire must be worn at all times* and *Refrain from grunting or profanity*. I'm not even sure what "proper attire" on a gym floor means. As for grunting and profanity, well, I think that's just fine sometimes. I see the enthusiastic trainer with her clipboard head to the reception area, looking for me. I'm already waiting outside the small office where she will do the assessment. Here I am, here I am. My Oz is invisible, but I am not.

"There you are!" "There you are!" She sees me. "I thought you might have forgotten our appointment," the trainer says. She extends her hand and introduces herself. She tells me not to be nervous.

"It's a big step to have one of these assessments; it takes a lot of courage."

But I'm not nervous. I don't feel like it's a big step at all, and I'm not sure why doing this assessment would be consid-ered courageous.

"I just want to find out where I'm at in terms of strength... y'know?"

"Sure thing, sure thing."

A body composition analysis is included in the assessment session. I step onto a fancy scale with hand grips. I don't feel a thing, but this tidy machine spits out a piece of paper that represents what's going on inside my body. It's broken into categories: under, normal, over. The trainer hands me the sheet with the kind of drawing you'd see on a commercial for over-the-counter pain medication. It shows me how my muscle is distributed in my body. Seems okay. A few physical tests will allow the trainer to place me on a continuum: under, normal, or over. I have to perform a squat and while she watches me, I guess how old she is. Maybe thirty years younger than I am?

"Your glutes are really tight. How old are you?"

"Fifty-eight."

"No! You're not!? Do you use a lot of creams?"

"Well, sunscreen."

"You have such a baby face," she says to me.

IV. Hair and cartilage

"D'you like your ears?" the stylist says, her shark-tooth-sharp scissors poised over my right ear.

"Uh, I guess so."

"I'm only asking because if you like your ears, I'll cut above and around them and just keep trimming." My hair, or my ears?

"I'd like to keep my ears," I say. The stylist doesn't smile.

I dropped into this discount hair salon because I want a cheap, quick trim. Before this, after first deciding to go grey, I'd gone to a barber a couple of times. I wanted my hair cut à la Tilda Swinton, buzzed on back and sides, long on top. I'd had my hair cut by barbers in my twenties during my punk phase. One even made sure to shape a pair of little sideburns in front of my ears. I liked the sideburns. I liked my ears. I also liked the way the short bristle on my neck and the back of my head felt. My hair was jet-black back then. I lined my eyes jet-black, too.

I spotted my first grey hair when I was twenty-eight and pregnant with my eldest son. It squiggled up from my head like an antenna tracking more of its kind. I yanked it out. When there seemed to be more grey hair on my head than black, I started to dye it. A dark reddish brown for a long time. Followed by a brief flirtation with blonde because the grey roots weren't so apparent as they grew out. Grey wanted to take over, and I reached a point where I was happy to let it. I'd never believed in black-and-white answers—living life in a grey area has always been my thing. Now my hair matches the place I like to be—open to infinite possibility in a place where choices and situations are never black and white. I distrust blue, cloudless skies in the heat of summer. I like grey, over-cast skies. The comfort of close clouds. I feel there's some expectation that I should be deeply affected by "letting my hair go grey"—but I'm embracing this changing colour. It is soft and comforting.

My ears, which I like, are just cartilage covered with skin. My nose is cartilage, too, but a nose is different. I've always thought it was too big. Both my ears and my nose will get bigger as I age, I'm given to believe. What about my knees? Cartilage is critical to knees, with the joint complication (no pun intended) of bone added to the mix. My knees aren't getting bigger, as far as I can see, but they are becoming very unforgiving. They hurt after spin class sometimes. I sit on a chair, with my leg propped on another chair and a bag of ice on my knee. I think of how beneficial the ice is, shrinking the swollen cartilage, or whatever is hurting. The ice will help the pain in my knee. The thought crosses my mind that an ice cube in a gin and tonic might be more beneficial, might make me feel better.

I am here. I am happy. This body is mine. I do have a soul. I feel it. In my bones.

The Roxy Project

CECELIA FREY

THE FIRST TIME I saw Roxy, it was a Tuesday. ABBA was pumping on the soundtrack to the tune of "Dancing Queen," the aerobics instructor was chanting, "knees up, one and two and three and four," twenty pairs of legs of various dimension in various garb were moving in various patterns and sequences. Late as usual, I rushed into the gym and made ready to hop up and down and sideways in my usual spot, only to find that I couldn't. Someone was in my space!

Skinny legs in black tights topped with two large rounds of fleshy buttocks bouncing like beach balls, a filmy chiffon see-through top revealing jiggly arms as well as a black lacy bra, non-sport and noneffective, the whole topped with a bleached blonde frizz and a pink bow. On her feet were black ballerina slippers.

Who was this creature touch-stepping in my place?

Obviously, a newcomer, her getup shouting that she was not there for a serious workout. We Over 50s are a class of middle-agers or early old-agers, mostly in baggy jogging pants and T-shirts discarded when the kids left for university or jobs. For some of us that was a long time ago. I'm still wearing Leonard Cohen's "I'm Your Man."

At our fitness centre, City Rec as we fondly call it, the same people have been going to the same classes for donkey's years (in my case, thirty-five to be precise, although back then I was in the Under 50s). We have various motivations in attending—weight control, well-being, social intercourse. For me, such activity has been and is absolutely necessary, in the beginning as an antidote to sitting for hours at a computer as a copy editor for a publishing firm and, later, in retirement, to spending hours in a reclining position awaiting visitation from the muse. I had always thought I would write a novel when time allowed, something along the lines of *War and Peace*. However, since I was already in my early sixties, a novel seemed like a poor investment of my time and energy. Thus, most afternoons found me comfy cozy in my recliner, writing board on knees, composing poetry.

On the whole, we in the Over 50s are a pretty close-knit group, having weathered and commiserated (with some degree of detachment while sitting on the hall bench changing boots for joggers or at after-class coffee) over deaths and divorces, heart attacks and slips on the ice or trips on the ironing cord, retirements to the coast or a care facility. When my partner passed a few years ago, I don't know what I would have done without the Over 50s. We get along well, and part of this getting-alonging is due to the fact that we all have our own particular happy place, our square metre of hardwood that to each of us is sacred, and everybody, EVERYBODY, knows that you do not take another's space on the floor.

Of course, from time to time, newcomers enroll who do not know this rule. That's all right. We're a civilized, tolerant bunch. Also, we have a method for dealing with this problem. With the ostensible purpose of doing a little pre-class stretching, we move in on the newcomer, sidling into our spot, forcing him or her, gently, to shift over a row into an otherwise unoccupied spot, which allows the old-timer to reclaim her rightful spot. Most people comply, either consciously or unconsciously, to this subtle soft-muscling procedure. Oh, once in a while things get dicey, but on the whole the system works well and nothing of a violent nature has taken place so far.

The first day I encountered the apparition I was later to know as Roxy, I decided to bite the bullet and ride out one class in the space directly behind her. Definitely, a one-timer, I told myself. She won't be back. Doesn't fit the fitness class profile. Hardly worth the effort of the manoeuvring it would take to move her. Already, I could hear her wheezing, and we weren't even finished the warm-up.

Events of the class corroborated my observation. She was totally uncoordinated with no sense of rhythm or anything else, for that matter. When the instructor said left right, she stepped right left. When the instructor said knees up, she did some sort of cross kick. Invariably, she was out of sync with the music. She seemed to be in her own little world, dancing to her own drummer, blithely unaware of the instructor or the people around her.

Which was all very well. Far be it for me to comment on the abilities of other people in the class. It was just that, being directly in front of me, she threw me off my rhythm and movements. I tried to ignore what was happening before my eyes but the amazing contours of her ample buttocks had a hypnotizing effect, as did the crazy steps of her ballerina slippers and her unsynchronized arm movements. I found myself following her moves, stepping left right when I should have been stepping right left, performing the shuffle instead of the grapevine. I couldn't fit myself to the beat of the music.

All in all, my workout for the day was severely compromised. My focus was so distracted, when her mound of hair threatened to topple, I stepped forward, hands outstretched, to catch it. When it didn't topple, I spent the remainder of the class anxiously anticipating the collapse. As we lowered ourselves to our mats for ab work and stretching, I heard beside me a sound resembling a street-cleaning truck picking up loose gravel, followed by a long aaarrrggghhha. I thought perhaps an ambulance should be called, but no one else in the class seemed to notice.

As we were hanging up mats and ropes, I could finally see her face—full makeup, including false eyelashes, obviously trying to obscure the fact that she was "a woman of a certain age" as the French say. "I'm here for my heart," she confided.

On the way home, I stopped at the supermarket to pick up a few things for supper. Standing in the express line, looking forward to home and my cup of tea, I heard a hack and cough and clearing of throat that already had tones of familiarity. I hoped it was one of those tricks of the mind, like a nightmare that inserts itself into your daytime consciousness, but turning in the direction of the disgusting sound, I saw that the person who called herself Roxy was directly behind me in the lineup. She smiled broadly in recognition, looked at my chicken pie, and croaked in a loud voice for all to hear, "You know, dear, those are loaded with calories..."

Cutting her off, I sucked in my stomach and made for the parking lot, feeling all eyes at three checkouts staring at my thighs.

When she showed up at Thursday's class, my heart sank, then hardened. I am by nature a gentle, easy-going person who deplores unpleasant situations, but I vowed to retrieve my happy place, if for no other reason than to be happy. I could not let myself capitulate to someone who was, in effect, stealing from me, stealing my place in class, stealing a piece of my life. At "Gimme a Man After Midnight," I made my move. At each touch and step I advanced forward, closer and closer into her space, which, of course, was my space. With each grapevine, I graped a little closer. With each knee up, I hopped a little closer.

She didn't seem to notice. I knew she was faking it. Two can play at this game, I said to myself. I pretended I didn't see her and caught her with my left arm flung out in a biceps curl. She didn't so much as blink. It was as though I wasn't there. I tried again. While engaged in an arm exercise, up/side/down/clap clap, I managed to wallop her shoulder with the out-flung side move. Again, nothing.

By the end of the hour I was almost resigned to moving to the other side of the gym. Then, I could actually feel my spine stiffen. Why should I move? She was the interloper. But wasn't the class itself more important than this old hag who threatened me with every awkward move, I argued back. Before the next class, this self-debate became pointless because she started stalking me outside the class! Library, drugstore, bank, at every venue embarrassing me with her loud voice and raucous laugh, her overly friendly behaviour, for she would talk to anybody. She would call across the street to people she didn't know but I knew quite well.

At this point I should say that I was a well-known fixture in the neighbourhood, having lived in it for forty years, arriving with my husband shortly after our marriage, raising our children here. I had a reputation to uphold. I couldn't be seen keeping company with this caricature of humanity who smelled!

At the supermarket, I hid in the frozen foods, at the drugstore between the walls of paper towels, at the library in the stacks. I found myself peeking around corners, waiting for her to leave. But, invariably, she found me, and when she did, she would announce, "Those frozen dinners are nothing but additives." Or, "Is that on the Weight Watchers list?" Or, "Fiery red! At your age! You gotta be kidding." Or, "You ought to be ashamed of yourself, reading that drivel. Get yourself a book with some artistic integrity for heaven's sake."

The last straw was the day when she turned to me after class with her smarmy smile and said in a condescending manner, "You're doing really well for your age." The gall of the woman! My age, indeed! She was at least ten years older than me.

What could I do to get rid of her? The answer came when at the start of a class, I happened to comment, "Here again, I see," and she answered with a peppy, "Oh yes, as long as I'm on two feet I'll be here."

The aha moment. What if she were not on two feet? What if she had an accident? Oh, nothing lethal, a small accident, just enough damage so that she could not come to class. As luck would have it, an opportunity arrived that very day. Roxy was walking alongside me as we left the building (of course she was, she stuck to me like crazy glue). We were crossing the icy parking lot when "what if" entered my mind, and before I knew it I was slipping sideways into her, throwing her off balance. As luck would have it, her hands reached out to me for support and down we both went, her on top, me underneath cushioning her blow.

The result was an unscathed Roxy and my twisted ankle, which, although I didn't appreciate it at first, turned out to be well worth the pain and inconvenience because it rid me of the woman. Yes, folks, I had to quit the aerobics class. While I could scarcely walk, I could still move my trunk and shoulders, so I started working upper body in the weight room, using machine weights, finishing with mat work and stretching. It was quite lovely. Peaceful, with the added bonus of ogling the hunks who were lifting weights around me, mostly young hunks but, what the heck, I was only looking.

Ralph was an old hunk. I guessed about seventy. He was in great shape. Tall, nice looking, great biceps and triceps, flat abs, no overhanging belly, great sense of humour, well spoken. He was retired from a career as a geologist and had also lost his partner in the recent past. Between sets, we started chatting. He liked being outdoors, liked hiking and looking for rocks. We talked about what to have for dinner when you're cooking for one. We exchanged recipes.

I started wearing makeup for my workout. I coloured my hair, bought new expensive wrinkle cream as well as the latest in trendy workout gear that smoothed things over and held all the loose flesh together in a tight package. I contemplated a face lift but decided that that would be too much bother. As it was, I looked pretty damn good with my new purchases and regime. Old friends wouldn't recognize me. I scarcely recognized myself! I knew that Ralph was on the verge of asking me to go for a coffee after our workout.

By now my ankle was healed, and I was on the treadmill, totally absorbed and ogling a young man who could only be described as eye candy, when a croaky voice like a magpie in heat came from the treadmill next to me, "You could be his grandmother, for God's sake!" followed by, "What have you done to your hair? Why are you wearing that silly disguise?"

Roxy had found me.

I looked quickly toward Ralph who was working his biceps on a nearby bench. Had he heard? He must have heard. Roxy, as usual, had not bothered to lower her voice, in fact, had raised it due to trying to be heard above the noise of the treadmill.

From then on, every time I wanted to have a conversation with Ralph, I found Roxy standing between us, talking incessantly about herself, bragging about her kids and grandkids, telling him about her recent trip to Barcelona. Since he was planning a trip to Spain, he was all ears to her suggestions and totally ignored me and anything I had to say. She found out that his favourite pie was lemon meringue and shared her generations-old recipe with him.

One morning after finishing my exercises, I found Ralph and Roxy in the lobby. He was helping her on with her boots! They were going for coffee!

I thought about returning to the aerobics class, since Roxy seemed to have abandoned it. But I had the sinking feeling that she would follow me. I had the hopeless knowledge that I could never get rid of Roxy. This knowledge was so demoralizing, I gave up caring. My habits and housekeeping skills went down the drain. I had always been neat, personal cleanliness and grooming important. I had always had an obsession with order and routine, Mondays for cleaning the kitchen, Tuesdays for laundry and ironing, and so on. Now, I found myself cleaning a kitchen cupboard at midnight or doing a load of laundry on Sunday. Sometimes I skipped the kitchen altogether. I stopped vacuuming unless I was expecting guests. I left books and papers lying on the floor, beneath the coffee table, stacked on the dining table. Dishes piled up in the sink. Most days I didn't get dressed until noon. One day I noticed a peculiar smell. After an extensive search for something gone bad in the fridge, I realized it was me.

My voice reflected the change. Old friends didn't recognize me when I answered the phone. Once cheery and upbeat, I became a croaky whisper.

One day, I dragged myself out to aerobics, only to find that Roxy was also there, in my spot of course. In watching her moves, I was surprised to see how she had improved since that first time. She followed the instructor, she actually kept time with the music. At the end of the class, I was lowering myself to the exercise mat when I heard a loud ahhhhh, indicating stiffness of joints, followed by assorted grunts and groans and realized that the sound was coming from me.

After class, I spotted Roxy bustling along the street, into the bank, the liquor store, the market, overall a bit wobbly, hobbly (she was favouring a hip), but *there*. She was heading for the hair salon for a touch-up. She'd had her cataracts done and boasted that no longer did she need eyeglasses. After the hair job, she had an appointment at Groovy Nails for a pedicure, manicure, and facial. Ralph was taking her out dancing.

Things were dark indeed. But, then, as so often happens, they got darker.

I had got out my writing board and pen, which had become an act of despair without expectations, a habit that I would have abandoned if not for the fact that the days contained a lot of hours that needed to be filled. I had made myself comfortable in my recliner, I had penned some words. I looked down at what I had written. I peered. I squinted. I could scarcely read the letters. They were so small. Teensy weensy. *I see you/bending over your skis/laughing.* What was that all about? I didn't remember writing anything about skiing.

After a few minutes during which shock gave way to disbelief, I told myself not to be silly. Write big! I commanded myself. My hand wouldn't do it! My hand would not obey my mind's command! *the cold air/in your red toque.* Where had those words come from? They weren't me. The writing wasn't me.

Needless to say, that was the end of any creative endeavour for the day. I must be ill, I told myself. Take two Tylenol and sleep it off, I directed myself. Things will be better tomorrow. But they weren't. The next morning, I got to my writing the minute I jumped out of bed, after a coffee, it goes without saying. My writing was even smaller than it had been the day before! The next week saw me in a fever of creativity, working to make my script larger, finding day by day that it was getting smaller. Soon it would disappear altogether. Soon I would disappear altogether. I was being erased. I knew that if I did not do something, I would cease to exist.

I thought it through. My situation must have something to do with Roxy. She had gotten into my mind. Her influence was destroying me. If my writing samples were any indication, there was not much time left.

I would have to kill Roxy. But how?

I was sitting at my kitchen table. How many murders, I wondered, are planned at kitchen tables? Lots, I'd bet. I became cold and calculating. For starters, I eliminated the impossible—knives, guns. Where would I get them and anyway I didn't know how to use them. Poison—how would I administer it? I supposed I could take up swimming. She would follow. I could drown her in the pool, push her under in the hot tub, turn up the steam in the steam room. I could entice her back to the weight room and trip her on the treadmill. But that would not necessarily lead to death, and with my luck I'd end up tripping myself.

Dropping into the fitness class, seeing her in the flesh, might help me determine the method. It was a Thursday, ABBA was again pumping on the soundtrack, this time "Super Trouper." Again I ran into the gym, late as usual, and took my usual spot with the instructor chanting, "grapevine, four steps left, four steps right." I was well into the second grapevine when I realized *I was in my own spot*! Where was Roxy? Believe it or not, I had a moment of regret, of loss, you might say. I had been pumped with my murder plans. I felt like a deflated balloon. She'll be back tomorrow, I assured myself.

But she was not back tomorrow or the next day or the next. Roxy had totally disappeared into the ether. I inquired of other people in the class, but they had no knowledge of who I was talking about. No one seemed to remember her.

I never saw Roxy again, except once. That was the day when Ralph and I were in the mall on our way to our favourite coffee place. I looked up quickly and there she was! Heading straight for me, striding with confident swinging gait. I blinked hard, twice. She was still coming. It must be the cataract operation, I decided. I could see too clearly. Panic took hold. I knew she would comment in front of Ralph about my drooping eyelids, my flapping jowls, my dye job that was overdue, details that had recently shouted at me from my bathroom mirror. She was a few strides from me. We were closing in on each other, from opposite directions. There was no escape.

Just in time, clarity asserted itself. I felt my strength. I knew what I had to do. I took a deep breath, squared my shoulders, sucked in as best I could, closed my eyes and held my arms wide. I took the final fatal step, embracing Roxy, carrying her with me along the length of the mall and beyond.

Rarification

VIVIAN HANSEN

THE CRONE GAZES BACK AT ME, her face drooping at the jowls, crinkled rows around her eyes. She needs to shave her chin every day and can only see to do it in a brightly lit bathroom mirror. She wears bifocals, but these have sat on her face for twenty years now. Once, when her younger self was involved with the wrong man, she desired more than was hers. Then she could not look at herself in the mirror. Since then, she has made the necessary journey toward forgiving her weaknesses and lack of wisdom. In this mirror, she can encounter and evaluate her face, and that is a gift of her age.

The image is mine, I own this crone. I no longer dress her up. I no longer menstruate; I haven't since my fiftieth year. I may have mourned my loss of reproduction and permission to disengage with the world, but now the world no longer desires me. Life is now dry enough to ruminate on the vagaries of decisions—my own and others'. Oddly enough, the world doesn't seem to care what the crone thinks. Perhaps it never did, long before I could call myself a crone. And what do I know of slight goddesses anyway? My moon time always gave me a false sense of security, reminding me that I was still able to reproduce, to care for and nurture children.

Premenopausal me could fight armies and anyone who challenged my nest. The reflex of caring for a mate was no more than a shrug, a must-do choice to uphold that nest. Now the nest is my own, and I am the only one who wishes to live here. I am satisfied with the ascetic vision of silence and contemplation. There is no one here. I am warm. My cats sleep with me.

Once, as an adolescent, I menstruated when it was not convenient. The blood factor exposed me in a way that it cannot anymore. Almost fifty years after this experience, and now that I live my life as a crone, I thought I might look back on menstruation and its locus of meaning for me. One would think that after all these years I would write about pregnancy, reproduction, perimenopause and the angry edema associated with premenopausal emotions. But it was this memory of menstruation, this incident of walking down the aisle of a church in my fifteenth year, that has sat in my mind.

Many years ago, I sent this small story off to Ronald Grimes, professor of Religion and Culture at Wilfrid Laurier University, who was collecting stories about ceremony and life passage:

I was confirmed when I was fourteen. I prepared for the ceremony, studied the meanings behind the faith, and memorized the creeds. The ritual was long practiced and well-rehearsed. The accoutrements were perfect; the special effects assumed a mystical importance. This was a Christian rite of passage.

I studied the rituals of the church every Thursday night for two years. Those years were formative. My breasts grew, my body made curves around my frame, and I tried to make sense of the present and future. I menstruated every thirty days, cried every twenty-one. No ritual existed to explain this cycle. Christ had no vagina. He bled only when he was nailed to the Cross. His suffering was final, while mine was chronic and apparently meaningless.

I was to be confirmed on April 23, 1972. My period arrived on April 21 along with its pain and fatigue and the introspection required by my imminent religious rite of passage. All day that Friday I hurt, my cramps rolling in waves over my abdomen. I prayed. I wept. I suffered. Outside, springtime emerged from the cold, unyielding ground, but the blooming crocuses, bluebells, and fragrant daffodils did not help my disposition or my physical, mental, and spiritual pain. I knew only the presence of my own body and the overwhelming power of its emerging force.

My brother teased me mercilessly when he found out that I was menstruating: "How are you going to walk up the aisle? All that blood will leak right through your white dress. Everybody will see it and laugh, especially the boys." I shrieked in frustration, mortified by the callous mockery I would get from the congregation.

My mother found me one night, weeping beside my bed for no apparent reason. "Girl, what's the matter?"

"I don't know where Jesus is. I try to talk to him, but he's out of reach. I want to take communion on Sunday, but I want to be with him first." She had nothing to say. How could she know, after all, where they had lain him?

I resolved nothing. Saturday was spent bleeding and musing over the echoes of my brother's vulgar comments. Sweat dripped from my brow, and I took frequent baths to rid myself of the filth. I hoped to stem the tide of blood, tears, and misery.

Nothing helped. I showed up at the church in a short white lacy dress and walked down the aisle, the bleeding bride of Christ. I felt my brother's eyes on my back. I felt as crucified as if the crowds had nailed me. I knelt at the altar, ready to be transformed, to experience the power of communion.

"The Body of Christ, given for you." I felt the biscuit melt in my mouth, drying and searing my tongue.

"The Blood of Christ, shed for you." The red wine merged with the host, helping me to swallow the body. All I could think of was the mortifying fear that my own blood would show and efface the ceremony, erasing the perfection.

The ritual over, I sneaked into the bathroom, assuring myself that I had padded all the shameful parts. No blood showed. The ceremony was complete. My endometrium was concealed, the rite of passage complete.

My confirmation happened just that once. I have pictures of my white virgin self, my smooth and supple young body smiling into a camera lens. That girl is triumphant, because her menstrual pad worked when it should have. I suffered through the rites and performed my religious commitments, but they required me to exclude the reality of my own body.

After this piece was published, I received an email from a woman in Ontario who had been ordained in the Lutheran Church. She wanted to speak with me about a ceremony to be "de-ordained," and she believed I could help her. Her quest troubled me; I did not believe I was the ascetic guru at the top of the mountain who could guide her religious abdication. What troubled me most was that my text of spiritual tensions had been appropriated and assumed a significance that I could not foresee. In exposing my blood, I had called out to the world, to an audience I did not know.

Dr. Grimes, the editor, commented on my work, calling it an example of "rarification"; an "initiatory trouble." The message of rarification is "the detachment of a rite from its physiological roots." He provided an analysis of my blood flow, and its privacy was no longer mine to guard:

In much of the European- and Christian-influenced West, not only are rites of passage out of sync with social and biological rhythms, but contradictory messages are structured into the rites themselves. The result is a double bind, a message received spiritually and biologically that says, in effect, "Do this. Don't do this. And don't speak about the contradiction between the two messages." In telling the story, Vivian slices through the double bind. She articulates the contradiction between being urged ritually to embrace the redemptive qualities of blood while, at the same time, having her own most persistent relation with blood, menstruation, liturgically denied. A religion of incarnation—one that declares that God became flesh and that hopes for the resurrection of the body—conveys the tacit message, "Flesh and blood are suspect. Let flesh and its desires not be mentioned; let blood and its stains be hidden."

As a menstruating woman of fourteen, I felt betrayed by the rarified need to hide my flesh. The white dress would only allow the betrayal to seep through. There was no garment I could wear to hide my female state. In this critique, I had been exposed, but I had to own the passages. They traversed through the authority of my personal narrative. My passion in blood would pursue me as it does any woman, for another forty years.

As I approach old age, I still carry around my womb, my muscle reminder of womanhood in its early years, and I consider the features of the crone. She is elder, wise, often angry, and does not back down from a fight with anyone who obstructs justice and compassion. I like this woman. She no longer bleeds, and so she no longer risks the condemnation that is inherent in exposure. I like the way I have shriveled into the effigy of a crone. I like what I can accomplish within the church, with a new sense of suspicion of its weaknesses to embrace women and anyone who holds marginal identity. My crone wisdom allows for grace and its redemptive path.

I have a daughter and a grandson. Imparting the wisdom of my ages has been a great blessing to me, affirming my female place in this world. I am a practicing Christian, but I had not been going to church from ages twenty-one to forty-five; coincidentally, the period of production and reproduction. This is the demographic where a woman is most likely to experience that double bind of rarification; where menstruation assumes an enormous role, removing her from public production as well as spiritual connection. At least, the spiritual connection that requires performance in organized religion.

Let blood and its stains be hidden. When we actively pursue this social norm, this notion applies not only to menstruation, but also to the redemptive role of a risen Christ. It applies to those people who work actively in treating illness and disease, as well as soldiers whose essential war strategies lead to a consuming knowledge of blood. When blood and its stains emerge from the white dress, humanity emerges from silence. I wonder if my emergence from forty years of menstrual and sexual silence is related to the end of blood. I would rather that the church acknowledged blood—human blood as well as God's blood. Perhaps this is the point— and why I now feel strangely safer in the church than I had in my youth. Perhaps this is part of why Christ encourages us to look after widows and orphans—woman and children who exist on the margins of power. That power is so highly suspect: it effaces blood.

I wrote a poem in my middle years when my natural power was strongest, bleeding into the earth at my menstrual time:

Finishing June

Thunder unrelenting,
zippered lightning flashes
one week after Summer Solstice.
Poetry waiting for words,
like rain opening.
Thunder peeling—like a noisy lover.
Thor's roared laughter—a shout of sacrament.
Haunching naked, wet.
Forgetting letters that draw
from me, a different intelligence.
Obsessions counting rain.
too many drops
to measure my cells, holding pain.
Knowledge seeps, ebbing from
the urge of the Solstice,
a week after time
                    tempers my mettle.

I am sensuous, slipping
bare toes
bush and breasts
drenched and dripping
under my May Day tree.
and 4 o'clock in the morning,
an hour before robins sing
or chickadees chrrrr,
minutes before menstruation,
blood marks the end of obsession.

Leaving June,
I am one year and 40.

But what, indeed, do I know of a slight goddess? As I enter a church these days, either for worship or outreach, I enter as a crone. Oddly enough, the nature of corporate religion finds the crone's appearance comforting. But taking her for granted could be dangerous to the status quo. Yes, she is physically vulnerable; she has no sex appeal. She does not bleed and therefore cannot be compromised. She does not take orders but filters a demand through the core of her wisdom before she acts. She speaks in whispers, or a low voice that murmurs. She points a craggy finger where something is wrong. She is not safe to those in power who might seek to oppress. She is no less powerful and disturbing for having survived beyond her moon time. In the muscle memory of blood, and the sacrifice of reproduction and nurturing, she recalls her full strength. Her blood has leached into the earth, into pews, into the workplace. She is no longer afraid of what seeps through the purity of a white confirmation dress.

LOVE

The Art of the Scarf

DEBBIE BATEMAN

MOST OF HER FRIENDS have worn scarves for years, thin silks in deep red and purple, thick cottons in turquoise, multi-layered weaves of wool in rust and brown. They roll lush textures into elegant shapes, letting their scarves hang in loose ties or coiling them around their necks.

Teresa has a lot to learn about the art of the scarf. Until recently, she'd only ever worn one under a winter coat to warm her throat, nothing so precious it couldn't be stuffed into an empty sleeve for safe keeping. Yet, recently, she spent an entire afternoon in boutiques, wrapping and unwrapping scarves around her neck, feeling the silk over her skin.

The day she has sex with Richard for the first time, she's wearing an apricot chiffon scarf with touches of white and turquoise. After she takes off her winter coat, the delicate fabric remains swooped over her chest. When she joins him at the coffee counter, it billows between them.

They'd snuck off to his apartment in the middle of the workday. As a diversion tactic, they'd decided to go for coffee afterwards. Anyone who happened to see them would think that was all they'd done, or so Richard claimed. But the huff of the espresso maker, the froth of the milk, the dark enticing scent of coffee remind her this is not something they should be doing. She's sure people can tell from the blush on her cheeks, the heat shimmering over her skin. When the barista asks her what she wants, she wonders, does he guess?

They sit in a quiet corner with a bookshelf on one side, a potted palm on the other. Away from curious onlookers, Teresa leans closer. A secret warmth glows inside her. Richard is ten years younger than she is. He's the dean of Information and Communications Technologies. She's his assistant. If anyone had told her this would happen, she'd have never believed them. She has been acting like a person she doesn't know.

Her family smiles on the photo standing proudly on her desk, and it's not like she's stopped loving her husband. On any given day Steve does countless things for her, making her sandwiches, washing her car, putting away the high-heeled shoes she kicks off when she comes through their door, buying her flowers. That very morning when they'd said goodbye, he'd hung her lunch bag over her shoulder and planted a loud kiss on her cheek.

Richard tips the wide rim over his mouth. A lock of sandy blond escapes onto his forehead. Pinching the paper tag, Teresa pulls out the tea bag from her mug and sets it on a napkin. She takes a sip and looks up. His attention returns to her face. The salmon-coloured sweater she's wearing fits well. The colour makes her cheeks look flushed, her lips fuller, and she's fairly certain it makes her look younger. Under the froth of her apricot scarf, the v of her sweater dips to reveal a hint of cleavage.

A grin widens under Richard's closely trimmed moustache. He leans across the small bistro table, strokes the scarf Teresa rewound around her neck after they'd had sex. "What's this?" he asks, gently tugging a loose end.

| When Teresa discovered streaks of silver on the innermost layer of the hair around her face, she boldly changed her style, rolling back her waves, bringing the underside into full view. The highlights added drama to her temples. The look made her seem more experienced, she thought. It was a delicate balance, made youthful enough by the raven black covering most of her head, the abundance of curl in her bob. At fifty-five, she was proud of her undyed head, how she seemed to be aging with grace.

The first time she found a grey curl between her legs, she thought it must be something else, maybe a loose thread or a stray hair from their cat Betsy. She had never expected the silver to spread to the private regions of her body, an invasive crop of ashen stalks like death itself taking root at the entrance to her sex. It did not seem fair. Only the possibility of proving herself wrong gave her the courage to find out for sure. She pinched the thick grey curl between her finger and thumb and yanked. Tears seeped from her eyes and she despaired for the next time she would have to uproot the evidence of her fading pigment.

Not one for injections or skin peels, she did take fastidious care of her skin. She moisturized morning and night, dabbed the cream over her whole face and neck, devoted herself to a strict regime of self-care. She'd seemed to be aging more slowly than any of her colleagues or friends, so when she noticed a loss of tension in intimate places, she wanted to deny what she saw.

She and Steve were getting ready to go to the Sunday afternoon symphony. She had on a black pencil skirt and a push-up bra. While she smeared cherry sparkle over her open mouth, his eyes slid down her cleavage. He kissed her neck and she brushed him away, ignoring the disappointed look that crept over his face.

As they were riding in the car to the concert, Teresa faced the truth. When she'd flipped the sun visor and opened the tiny mirror, she'd only wanted to make sure there weren't lipstick smudges on her teeth. But her attention lowered and that was when she saw. Her once silken breasts were puckered and slack, her flesh worn-out balloons, blown up and emptied too many times.

Not long after, she started wearing scarves.

| Her girlfriends were always telling her how lucky she was to have married a firefighter. She met Steve at a fundraiser for burn victims when she was seventeen. Immediately she fell for him, the tall man with tender blue eyes, dark brown hair, and an innocent face. His flat belly was trim within the uniform, his chest so wide. When he put his arm over her shoulder, she felt he'd never let anything harm her.

Anyone would say they have a good life together with a nice home and great kids. Mark is in his last year of law school and Jenny is working on a nursing degree. Now that the kids have moved out, Teresa and Steve can do things they'd have never done before.

Decades have passed since his mistake and they long ago made peace. They both understand what happened. Women throw themselves at firefighters. It's an occupational hazard, every bit as risky as the smoke and the post-traumatic stress and the crazy drivers who crash into emergency vehicles blocking accident scenes. The anchor for the local TV news with her big hair and shoulder pads had not been the only woman interested in Steve.

He'd rescued a nine-year-old girl from the upper floor of her home. Smoke billowing from the opposite side of the house, he climbed over the garage roof and in through the window. The TV station showed clips of him coming down the ladder with the girl draped over his shoulders. He had one arm hooked around her leg, both hands clasping her opposite wrist. They took more shots later of Steve next to a shiny red fire engine.

People love firefighters, Teresa realizes, but she'd hated the way the anchor looked at her husband when she held the microphone to his lips. Although the public information officer was at his side, the anchor preferred talking to Steve. He was still in his duty gear, the front of his jacket unzipped, his helmet and Nomex hood already set aside, his thick and wavy hair mussed around his intense eyes.

The next time the anchor saw Steve was in a bar. He was out with the guys on a day off. The anchor bought him a drink and begged him to recall every detail of the rescue. Teresa can well imagine the hero devotion, the sickening enthusiasm, the unbridled worship. In those days, Teresa was occupied with raising their children, she did not have time to massage his ego, and she expected him to focus on their family. Instead, he had sex with the anchor in the backseat of her suv in the parking lot. Teresa knows the particulars because she forced him to tell her. It only happened once—or so he said. Over the years, she'd learned to let go of the arguments and she'd accepted his version and they'd gone on to have a lifetime together.

On that cold winter morning some twenty years earlier, with the sun turning the sky orange, he'd come home from his night shift and he'd shared the shame he'd kept covered for days. Teresa was glad to see him, as she always was when he returned home safely. She was thinking they'd crawl into bed, snuggle under the warmth of their down duvet. She could use a nap. Their daughter had been fed and was asleep in her crib. Their son was watching cartoons.

Steve sat at the edge of the bed with his head in his hands. "I had sex with someone else," he blurted. "Nobody important. I was drunk."

She stared at the heap of dirty clothes on their bedroom floor, the T-shirts dampened with breast milk, the pants stained with spit-up, the pregnant-woman panties she still liked to wear. She told herself she had to start taking dirty clothes to the hamper.

"I'll never do it again, I swear. Please say you can forgive me."

| All those moments in his office, their knees touching under the desk. Working on the proposal for the applied degree in Global Information Systems, Teresa and Richard spend long hours alone. At first, he only looks at her when she's busy taking notes. She feels the shiver of his eyes on her chest. If she glances up, she catches him. Soon he doesn't bother hiding his interest. His gaze lingers on her face, slips below warm and silky. Call it a trick of lighting or the perfect use of camouflage, it doesn't matter which. At her age if she doesn't enjoy the attention, she may never get another chance.

Everyone on campus knows Richard's story, how his wife left him for another man. Such goings-on are hard to hide when everyone involved works at the same place. When he sends an invite to Teresa's calendar marked private, she accepts with a flick of a finger, then closes the calendar and looks away. A rush of heat prickles her face to think of what she's done. Inside, an almost forgotten stirring awakens. Around the base of her spine, where she splits in two, living things begin to turn and stretch and wiggle.

They take separate cars. She parks blocks away and sneaks down dusty alleys where the gravel strains her ankles and scratches the heels of her shoes, leaving black nicks and nasty brown smudges on the leather. So many students and instructors live in the neighbourhood. It's worth being careful.

After sneaking up the stairway, she stands in front of Richard's apartment, watching the elevator, prepared to rush down the hall if it stops on his floor. Although he doesn't answer her knock, the doorknob turns in her hand. Safely inside, she kicks off her tattered shoes and walks through the unlit apartment to the open bedroom door. Her feet sink into the bedding he tossed onto the floor before she arrived. He's waiting on the open sheet, his flesh warming the dimmed room, pink skin on a hairless chest.

She perches on the edge of the mattress, facing away from him. A woman her age, by now she must've had sex thousands and thousands of times, yet she feels awkward as a teenager, afraid to show her naked self, terrified of her urgent need to be touched, the blind hunger of her skin, how much she wants to kiss him.

He unwinds the frothy scarf, peels off her salmon sweater, unfastens the bra, and lets it drop onto her lap while he warms the exposed breasts. All that would keep her restrained is gone. She lies on the bed, flat with open arms, freer than she's been in longer than she can recall, younger too.

Before they begin, his arms straight, rising above her, Richard smiles. She closes her eyes.

| Most of the women she knows had other lovers while they were young, before settling down. Until Richard, she'd only ever been with her husband. She tells herself it was absolutely a mistake, yet completely understandable for her to be curious. Besides, she hadn't done anything Steve hadn't already done to her. In a way, it brings their relationship back into balance.

After she's been with Richard, she feels more generous toward Steve. She gives him frequent backrubs, seafood suppers, his favourite beer chilled in the fridge and hand delivered. Steve has always had a flirty smile, a slight show of teeth behind smooth lips. No wonder women swoon for him. She falls herself, years after she thought she'd never risk it again.

When he kisses her neck, she leans into him and moans. Her skin is alive to his touch. They both notice the difference and silently agree to keep their secret as only a couple married a long time knows how to do. He approaches with less caution, grabs her with greed in his hands. She clutches him closer, tugs on his hair.

The recent encounter with Richard replays in her mind. She cannot escape flashbacks, so intense it's happening again, only now with her husband. Late at night when his body has slackened, Teresa kisses Steve's shoulder, waiting for him to rouse and turn to her. She aligns with his strong frame in the darkness. Her uncovered self presses his, the warmth of his hand following the curve of her hips, coming to rest at the fullest part, holding abundance.

Afterwards, when Steve wears a grin, his face gleaming with sweat, Teresa can almost believe she isn't doing anything wrong.

| The second time they take the same car, slipping away late-morning when any students living in his building ought to be gone. She checks the street before going into the apartment, but she does not ruin another pair of shoes. As a precaution, they use the back stairway, her leading the way, him in open pursuit. When they reach his floor, they are both giggling.

In the hallway, the chase is still on, with her in the lead, always in the lead. He unlocks his apartment door and they jostle into the private world inside. He barely has time to take off his shoes when she tugs him toward the bedroom and pushes him onto the unmade bed. Tearing the clothing off his wriggling body, she nearly pops the buttons on his crisp new shirt. He waits naked while she peels off her clothes and lets them drop to the floor.

Eyes closed in a tight embrace with a body she does not know well, she forgets all the years she did not feel. She pretends the broken faith, the loss of her husband's protection, the separation between them never happened. Trust is not a thing so fragile. Sex with her husband is better than it's ever been, this is okay, what she is doing is not only for herself. Except skin has its own kind of memory, and it's thoughts of Steve that overtake her mind in the peak of the moment. How she likes the roughness of his touch when he's trying to be gentle. How his wide chest pressed near hardens her nipples. In contrast, Richard is so thin, she feels like she's hugging herself.

When she opens her eyes, Richard is watching. His pale face is vulnerable. A mouse-like whimper leaves his mouth. Too late Teresa wishes she'd looked away. She sees herself as if from a distance, cannot believe what she has done, does not feel she dishonoured herself because how can it be wrong to recover a vital part of yourself before it is too late, and yet she knows in her bones she has hurt this man naked beside her.

Richard pats her thigh. She rolls away and looks at her wristwatch. "We're late," she says, getting out of bed. Even before they left the office, she knew they'd be rushed to make it back on time for the faculty meeting.

She's into her bra and panties before he leaves the bed. He only gets up after she's started fixing her face. Leaning toward his dresser mirror, she begins to spread the cherry sparkle. She's not wearing her shirt. From where it rests on the table, her scarf offers no help. She's not at home, he's

163

not her husband and it's more than cleavage now. On the shiny surface of the mirror, her gaze creeps upward from her breasts to her neck where the skin sags and folds. She lifts her chin and the results are worse. Her skin is a tent and she's tightened the cords.

She's only covered half of her upper lip when he turns the ceiling light on.

"Isn't that better? You can see yourself now."

| One thing about Steve, he came forward of his own accord and admitted his mistake. Until she'd escaped Richard's bedroom, rushed back to work, and arrived at the faculty meeting with messed-up hair and the smell of a man who is not her husband, she hadn't realized how brave Steve had been. She understands now what he meant all those years ago when he said he hated himself.

As soon as she gets home from work, she throws her clothes into the washing machine and gets into the shower. A little while later, Steve gets home and finds her lying on the couch in front of the TV with a fleece blanket on top of her. He sits on the edge of the sofa. "What's up? You sick?"

She turns down the volume and drags herself into a sitting position. The fleece falls into her lap. "No. I'm fine. Got home early and decided to relax."

Leaning closer, he brushes his lips over the side of her head. She lifts her chin and kisses him. He tastes like coffee and the orange he has every afternoon. Her hand reaches for his cheek, rests gently there in reverence for what may soon be lost. She's no longer confused about whose flesh she's touching.

"Is something wrong?" he asks.

"No, no. I'm tired, that's all."

There was a time she would never have lied to her

husband. They'd shared all their secrets until the morning that he'd confessed what he'd done. She was used to seeing him with reddened cheeks and heavy eyelids. He came home looking ruined after most shifts. But the way his mouth sagged, the way his fearful eyes latched onto hers, she'd known it was more than exhaustion.

After he'd told her, she'd held a pillow to her chest. She'd sent him away and refused to allow him anywhere near her. He'd left without argument. Then he'd waited patiently, was waiting still, for her to forgive him. She'd made a marriage out of his efforts and all this time she'd not seen what she was doing. For years she'd allowed him to keep trying to regain her devotion. The car washes, the lunches, the gifts and the servitude, she would give all of it back.

He lingers at the side of the couch, does not seem concerned by the silence, his attention drawn momentarily to the TV. She tries not to change the rhythm of her breathing. Her pulse thumps in her ears, the sound dragging her deeper into panic. She should say something straightforward like *I had sex with someone from work. A stupid mistake. I wish it never happened.*

| A week later, Richard sends another private invite. Teresa's computer tings and she opens the email. Since the moment at his bedroom mirror when the lights came on, their interactions have been perfectly respectable, nothing you wouldn't see between any dean and their assistant. Without hesitation, she clicks the big X and the insinuation is gone. Rapidly, she's deleting the experience from her life.

The next day, Richard calls her into his office. Lately, their communications have all been at the reception counter where she works. This is the first time since they last slept together that he's asked to see her alone. She perches on the chair, tucking her skirt around clenched legs. A fresh pad of paper rests next to the pen in her hand.

Even when he rises from his desk, she avoids his face. It isn't until he passes alongside her that she begins to follow his movements and soon he is out of view. The paint on the spot of the wall where the photo of his wife used to hang is cleaner than everywhere else. He's never chosen to put something else up in its place. All those hours in his office and she never noticed before.

He walks behind her and the door clicks. After he returns to his desk, he reaches for her hand. Before they make full contact, she slips out from under his touch, backs out of her chair, goes to the door and re-opens it. She stands at the desk, waiting for instructions, ready to leave.

He sighs, removes his glasses, washes his face with open hands, then looks at her with such disappointment she almost wants to apologize. Without the shaping lines of his glasses, his eyes look old and tired, small within pockets of weary skin, crow's feet at their corners.

"What's wrong?" he asks.

"I can't do this anymore."

Softly, she turns and goes through the open door. Her brand-new shiny heels click over the linoleum floor. Richard never tries again.

| After Steve told her he'd been unfaithful, Teresa slept with her back raised against him. She wouldn't acknowledge his touch or attempts at conversation. She'd hand the kids over to him when it was time for their baths. Before turning off the light, she'd allow Steve to go to where Mark was tucked in and kiss him goodnight. She'd let him do the same thing with Jenny after she was settled in her crib.

things, like their new nightly ritual. Time for bed, she'll say, before hitting the stairs. He'll follow close behind. Any faster and they'd be running. Her feet barely land on the carpeted stairs. His hot breath reaches out, worms down the back of her neck, makes her hurl her body forward. She always gets caught.

They undress on opposites sides of the bed. He unbuttons his trousers, opens his zipper. She gradually unwinds her black silk scarf, turns down her eyes, afraid to be vulnerable but yielding to that urgent need to be touched.

They meet on the marriage bed, embrace on cool beige sheets, the bedding tossed aside. Her nipples feel nothing under the cushioning bra she does not remove. Steve's face is blank. He does not whimper. He never realizes his wife is watching or that sometimes she thinks of some other man with curly blond hair not so different from Richard's.

Afterwards, they rest with legs intertwined. She turns her cheek to his chest. Her drooping eyes barely focus, yet she catches the silver glistening. She'd never noticed before the salt and pepper matching the hair on his head. Her eyes travel the length of his torso, linger at his groin, confirm her suspicions. Ever changing with the light, all she has to do is shift the angle of her head and the hairs turn dark. For a moment, it doesn't seem possible, but she rolls her head back to the resting position and the glint of silver returns.

She Will Drive

LISA MURPHY LAMB

SHE WILL DRIVE because her friends will drink too much. Keys, check. Reliable Natasha, check. Lights off, check.

Natasha (mostly) gave up drinking six months after the end of her marriage. Ted, her ex-husband, drank largely when she first met him (at a bar, no less). She liked him immediately. He was clever and funny and tall, and she adored his late-night antics—the way he helped her get over her worries, the way he was drawn to her and let her know it. Now, twenty-four years later, well, Natasha knows very little. She knows that living alone she must lock the door, so she does, walks toward her car, turns back up the sidewalk, checks the lock again.

| The cocoa furnishings of the bistro make her feel as she does at almost-fifty: drab, unexciting. So she drapes her bandhani scarf over the back of her chair and sits, hoping its explosion of colour roses her cheeks, distracts from her weight gain; ten pounds since their last get-together. Always the first to arrive, she checks her watch, then the door. She sees Tyler.

Tyler's pace quickens when he sees Natasha, and she stands to greet him. He scoops her easily into his arms and, for a moment, she forgets all her misgivings as her feet leave the floor. "Hello," he breathes into her hair, "it's good to see you."

Natasha falls readily into his embrace. "You too," she whispers back into his shoulder, then straightens. Tyler has been around longer than her marriage, and here he is still, here they are still.

Natasha knew Tyler years before she met Ted, but Ted she married. It was a good marriage and then, without an incident she can pinpoint, she and Ted were enemies. But none of this can matter tonight. Tyler is here.

He pulls out the chair beside her and sits. "It's always good to see you," he says.

"Is it?" She asks, but she knows it is, for this holds true for her as well.

"Always," he repeats. "Can I order you a drink?"

She nods and lets him know what she wants.

"A beer and a club soda," he says when their server appears at the table, "and where can I hang my jacket?" Tyler rises. The server extends her hand as he shrugs the jacket from his shoulders.

When the server returns, it's not with drinks but with a chair. Natasha protests. "There will just be the four of—"

Behind the server and her chair are Hetty and Evan and a stranger who relies entirely on the two of them to keep her upright. Eyes slits, lips slightly parted.

"Tyler, my man." Evan lets go of the girl in a rush to bear hug his friend. The girl slumps, head rolls violently to the left. Natasha hurtles forward to help.

"Hetty?"

"Just grab her. And don't make a scene."

Natasha helps deposit the girl in the seat newly placed at the end of the table.

The four of them sit. Tyler leans across the table, kisses Hetty full on the lips and then asks again, "What are we drinking? And what is her story?"

The server returns with the soda and beer.

"Two vodkas. Doubles. Rocks. Oh, and a water."

Natasha removes the straw from the glass, thinks of turtles and oceans, for how can she not? And places it on her bread plate.

"So, go on. Tell us the story of your little threesome." Tyler sinks back into his chair and puts the beer to his lips.

Evan speaks first. "Now, don't go thinking the worst. This is all Hetty's doing."

Natasha looks towards the girl. She is younger than them. Early twenties, likely. Wearing a blazer with a thin shirt beneath. Considering she cannot keep her head up, she looks good like only girls in their twenties can, even when comatose.

Hetty leans in closely. "We were walking here from the train. And there she was. Slumped on a bench. Passed out. We walked on but I couldn't leave her. So I dragged Evan back."

The server returns with the drinks. The four stop talking until she's gone, watch her leave. Her server uniform, a black dress, fits tightly across her backside. Her heels are high, though by law, she's no longer mandated to wear high heels.

"I tried to rouse her. Couldn't," Hetty continues.

"So?" Tyler says, "Your concern, Het?"

Hetty looks to Natasha. "Something bad's gone on. Someone's chewed her up and spit her out."

"She looks good to me," Tyler says.

"Exactly. I couldn't leave her to be preyed upon by someone with bad intention." Hetty thumbs in Evan's direction. "I've been around this one too long."

173

"What's the plan?"

"We'll buy her some soup. Sober her up. Give her bus fare and send her on her way."

"Look at you, Mother Hetty," Tyler says, sits back. "I like this look on you, though I can't quite square it."

"I'd want the same if this were my daughter."

Evan raises his voice and speaks deliberately to the slumped figure when a gargled noise leaves her lips. "Hey. You're not going to get sick, are you?" He sits back, punctuates his words.

The server returns, hears this. "She's not, is she?"

Evan replies coolly. "This may be my niece's last meal out. We're just not sure how long—"

"Oh," the server fumbles with the menus before handing them out. "Tonight's special is pied de porc pané. The chef simmers the pig for hours, debones it, then seizes what remains in a delicate golden crust. It's an ancient French classic. Let me know if you need anything."

The four let her leave.

"Cheers." Tyler raises his glass. "To old friends."

Tyler catches Natasha's eye as Natasha puts the club soda to her lips, looks across the table at her two long-time friends. Hetty and Evan were once a pair. Maybe still one. They were a pinup fantasy couple once, both are still vaguely pretty. Both are damaged, he by drugs and she by her devotion to him. They stay together because of Moppy, a girl they had twelve years ago.

Natasha lost her interest in watching Ted drink. Hers became a marriage of drunken scenes where one or both of them would storm out of restaurants and bars after a fight. Fifteen years in, Natasha was drinking nightly. Drink was the only activity she and Ted had in common by then, so she said yes when he asked if he could make her a drink. Cocktails didn't keep them together, though, like they do Hetty and Evan. Natasha looks at her friends sitting side by side with their vodkas.

"You two have always been the Devious Duo." Natasha tips her glass their way. "But this, this seems a bit." She looks around.

"Of an adventure? Yes, an adventure!" Evan says. Evan finishes his vodka in a dramatic gulp and looks around, glass in hand.

"Here's to the four of us," Natasha continues the toast. "I'm happy we're able to get together yet another year."

"And to our new-found friend," Hetty adds.

| Natasha stares at her plate. On it sits a mushroom the size of an infant's head. A mushroom the like of which she has never seen in this city before and, she knows, has travelled farther than the recommended 100-kilometre diet. She bends to smell the mushroom, press it. She sticks her fingers in its deformed holes like she is going to bowl it, licks her fingers and nudges her wine glass towards Evan. "I'll have a half-glass, please."

Hetty spoons soup into the waif's mouth before tasting her own starter. "When her head rolls to the left, I get a glimpse of Mickey Rourke." Hetty tucks a napkin into the girl's shirt. "We should name her Mickey, make her part of our little gang."

Tyler raises his glass. "Here's to Mickey." The three also raise their glasses Mickey's way, take a drink. Natasha attends to her mushroom, forgets Mickey.

"So. Hetty. What is your latest scheme?" Tyler puts his knife down after taking a bite.

"I'm ass-deep in writing my autobiography."

"Oh ho! Your life is so interesting that you have a book already? What has happened since our last meal and why wasn't I invited?"

"Do you not think being with this guy hasn't brought some drama to my life?"

"Suppose. What do you think about this, Ev?"

"It's a mind-fuck, really."

"And Moppy?" Natasha looks up from her mushroom appetizer long enough to ask. "She will be okay with a tell-all about her parents' lives?" Natasha looks towards Mickey and feeds her another spoonful of soup.

"Yes. Well, I've considered her."

"Well done, dear." Evan leans over and kisses Hetty, then drinks some wine.

"So, I've made some changes."

"Changes. To your lifestyle?" Tyler signals the server to bring another round of drinks.

"No. My autobiography."

Mickey coughs and Natasha puts the glass of water to her lips but can't make her drink. "Even The Comatose One realizes the absurdity of your statement." Natasha eyes Hetty.

"You can do that?" Tyler puts his knife down again and takes a second bite.

"What?"

"Make changes to your life story?"

"I told you it's a mind-fuck." When the server returns Evan raises his empty glass and welcomes another vodka. "Oh, what is young Mickey doing now?"

The four look over and Mickey's eyes flicker. "Hey," Hetty says, "wake up."

But that is all Mickey has in her. Two eye flickers.

"I hope this girl doesn't have any allergies," Hetty says while spooning some tomato bisque in her mouth. "If Picasso painted a Cubist self-portrait, nobody would say it didn't look like him, would they?"

"What the fuck are you on about now?" Evan's voice thunders across the table.

"My autobiography. Tyler wants to know if I can alter the events to protect you and our darling daughter. I believe I can. Make it an abstract, a Cubist rendering. Like a Picasso. Don't you think?"

"That's a jolly justification, Love. How are your hand-pulled noodles?"

"And you, Evan, what is new with you?" Tyler leans into the table, reaches across and takes a noodle from Hetty's plate. Natasha nudges her mushroom his way, but he waves it off.

"Oh, the usual bullshit. Lucky in business. Had another whale of a year."

"When are you going to fund one of my projects, then?"

"Oh, that old conversation."

"Yes, that old conversation. If you're going to keep putting the money up your nose, at least throw some my way. You still are putting money up your nose?"

"Yeah." He laughs. "I should stop, though. I'm getting old and it's taking a toll."

"Good. Then with that extra million. Put it in the arts. Put it in *my arts.*"

"Feh."

"You're a bastard, you know."

"A bastard with a new patch of grass."

"That's fucking newsworthy." Tyler tastes his veal tongue salad. "It better be that you revitalized an inner-city lot for kids."

"No! Better than that. Isn't it, Hetty?"

"What? Do you think someone fed her a roofie?"

"Of course, she's been roofied. But tell them about my patch of grass."

"Oh, God no. It's boring. Ask Tyler about his latest film or Natasha about her...Her what? What is it you are up to, Nat? Finally left The Bay and become a civil servant?"

Natasha wipes the butter slowly off her face. "Grass? I want to know more. Really." Turning to Tyler she speaks to his hair, his thick glorious hair that he has not lost over the decades. "Are you actively working on a film?" She once had a small part in one of Tyler's films, back in high school in his basement. She wonders what happened to it.

She hates that Tyler sits at her right side, her ugly side. She should have thought things out more closely when she arrived. Up until about a year ago, she hadn't considered all her flaws. Ted had whispered during a fight that no one would ever want to see her naked. During a fight about what? It didn't matter. Since that fight, that comment, she has spent many hours in front of the mirror wondering what happened to her.

"I like to sleep on the patch of sod in the courtyard in the middle of my house, well, backyard." Evan is telling his grass story. Natasha turns to him to listen, places her hand under her chin, then to the side of her face, sits straight, tightens her stomach muscles. She can't decide if she should surrender to the evening, trusting old friends, or keep aware of what she needs to do to look just that much more toned, that much less jowly, that much less almost-fifty.

"In the middle of Mount Royal, a block off the rowdy beer crowd and the roaring traffic?" Tyler asks.

"Yes. My favourite pub is mere steps away but I'm happy there, stretched out on my piece of turf."

Hetty makes a noise like she agrees. Natasha looks her way. The look on her face is an ugly one. She watches as

Hetty reaches across the table and slaps Mickey on her left cheek. Natasha startles. Mickey's eyes flicker and she speaks. "My aunt," she says and then the rest of her words tumble into the telltale glossolalia of a drugged mind. She tiptoes back into her slumber.

"Once a cop came to arrest me for being drunk and disorderly, but that night I wasn't. I was just choosing to sleep there."

"A goddamn patch of grass? A goddamn patch of grass!" Tyler remarks.

Hetty joins in. "It is. It's a goddamn piece of grass. I've seen it with my own eyes. He sleeps alone on the green square while I sleep alone in the bed upstairs."

Natasha looked towards Hetty. They are still together. Every year it is a different tale.

"This is what you have to tell us after a year?"

"It is a glorious section of grass. I piss on it like a dog. I commune with my patch of grass and it makes me happy. Do I not deserve to be happy?"

All four reach for their glasses. Natasha considers his happiness. Of course he deserves to be happy, they all do. He has a way of dancing through the decades, though, untouched, living still as she knew him in university. Natasha wishes her appetizer mushroom were bigger and that there were more left on her plate. So little makes her happy these days, but this mushroom is thrilling.

"You are a piece of shit, Evan. You have all this money and you won't give me a goddamn cent and you come to this dinner eating your pig snout on greens and telling us about your patch of grass like you've discovered the cure for restless legs syndrome." Tyler drains his glass and searches for the bottle but Hetty has just emptied it. Natasha looks for the server and gives her the nod. Again she looks to Mickey then spoons her another mouthful of soup. Mickey opens her mouth and swallows it. The soup is done.

"Restless legs syndrome?"

"Sometimes I get it. I'd like a cure."

Hetty asks, "Tyler. Tell us about your film. Evan, pay attention. Find out what us artists do. Important work."

"There needs to be more wine."

"I've ordered it," Natasha tells Evan. He looks bored already with his glass empty and the story of his patch of grass already told. "And here she is."

"You might as well bring another," Evan says.

"How were your appetizers?" the server asks, and begins to clear the dishes.

"Fine," Natasha quickly answers as she can tell her friends are drunk and agitated. "Delicious, really. Perhaps we could have another order of the lobster knuckles."

The server, balancing now five dishes, nods. Her left earring is caught up in her dark hair and Natasha wants to tell her but changes her mind. She's never been a mother but knows she'd come across as motherly.

"She's lovely looking," Hetty comments. "Remember when we were lovely looking, Natasha? Although we didn't know it as the twenty-somethings know it now. Instagram and all." Hetty pulls out her phone. She checks it. Then says, "Evan, tell us we're still lovely looking."

Evan leans over and kisses Hetty's hair. "You're both radiant as ever."

Tyler throws his arm around Natasha. "I disagree," he says. "They are more beautiful today than the day we met them."

"Fund his movies," Natasha says before he takes his arm away, she wants him to want to keep it there.

"Do you have a project on the go?"

"Only in here." Tyler points to his head. "Because my rich friend is an asshole and won't fund me."

"Get a job." Evan excuses himself from the table.

"I've got a job, Natasha." Tyler tightens his arm around her. "You know it. But supervising a group home does not fund my dreams."

Natasha sinks into the chair. The drink has made Tyler soft. His shoulders curve, his eyes turn down at the edges. He looks like a boy and an old man at once. Natasha yearns to lean in but then recognizes her erratic breath, remembers the post-divorce texts with him. Remembers Tyler is adorably mean, has always been, at least when it comes to the two of them. Natasha ended a marriage with a man who she met when he was adorable and left when he turned mean. So she's cautious with Tyler this time because she knows he holds both traits at once. Natasha can't resist him, though she's learned to be smarter. She pulls away.

"You'll do it."

"Yeah I will."

"The problem with French cuisine," Hetty announces from across the table, phone in hand, "is the small portion size. I'm starving."

"Our poor little raptor," Tyler says. "Oh, Hetty, what is so important that you must have that phone at the table?"

"Oh, you know I love you all, but you're not enough. I have to see what else is going on in the world. When Evan gets back, let's take a picture."

Tyler pushes her phone away. "Honestly, Hetty. Do that at home when you are alone."

"Back me up on this, Tash."

"I agree with Tyler. I rarely use my phone now."

"C'mon. You can't avoid it."

"Instagram is not my friend."

"More wine?" Tyler raises the bottle, but Natasha says no.

Evan sits down. He brings an extra layer of energy with him. "What's the story?"

"Natasha wants to post our picture on Instagram."

"No, I don't," Natasha says. "I actually don't have my picture taken anymore."

"No, why not?" Evan's voice is loud.

"Just don't like what I see these days."

"Oh, piss off to that," Hetty says.

"Also, I don't care to see Ted's Instagram photos of him and his new lover on their beach holidays."

"Darling, can you please pass the lobster?" Evan pulls the dish towards him and cuts a portion. "All the more reason to get your beautiful face out there with us. Let him be jealous."

Natasha watches Evan chew. "I'm not jealous."

Hetty reaches over for Natasha's hand. "Of course you are. He's dating someone ten years younger."

"Don't be a shit, Hetty," Evan says.

"What? He's a fool for letting this one go, but I'll bet she wears a bikini in the photos."

"She does." Natasha laughs.

"We're all assholes. All men are assholes," Evan says, his voice so loud that everyone in the bistro looks their way.

"No, he's a fucking asshole, for hurting our Tasha," Tyler says, "and such a cliché to date a woman who works for him."

"Cliché and illegal."

"Maybe his next Instagram post will be from jail."

Their laughter catches the attention of the entire room. It is a drunken, out of control, hysterical laughter and Natasha joins right in. It is completely true. Ted is a fucking asshole and she loves her friends more for being on her side.

And the entrées have arrived.

| "I am getting tired of Mickey at our table." Hetty's head is lolling back and forth, studying the face of their silent fifth dinner guest. Hetty's own curls, blonde, dance with the movement. For years Hetty's hair had been frizzy, but with age, she has learned to tame the curls into large coils. Her freckles, once concealed with too much makeup, now dot her skin with a carefreeness that has counteracted the effects of years of late nights and smoky lungs. And yet, there has been no one else but Evan.

"Your motherly instincts are precious."

"Moppy has life. Mickey's pissing me off. And there is not enough food on my plate."

"You are the size of a twelve-year-old and you eat like a linebacker."

"It's the drugs. Bad for every other part of me, except my weight."

Natasha has not yet picked up her fork. She's lingered over the essence of the beet sorbet and the sight of the purple stain against the snowy white of the arctic char. Natasha, too, is tired of Mickey, has been from the beginning of the night. These meals are sacred. Mickey has been the first to join their foursome, even Ted didn't join in during the years of marriage, nobody's spouse has. Natasha picks up her fork. She cuts a piece of fishy flesh and puts it in her mouth. All is forgotten. All is forgiven.

| "I can't believe this kid. She's out like a bear." Soft snores unfurl from Mickey's lips.

"Do we buy her dessert? Is that the polite thing to do?" Natasha asks.

"Soup went unappreciated."

"God. I'm sick of the sight of her," Hetty says. "Tash, help me. We'll take her to the bathroom and splash her face. See if that helps."

| "I'm tired." Rummaging through her purse, Hetty turns her back to Natasha who is wiping the water off Mickey's face. Mascara has smudged, but eyes remain closed, she stands because Natasha props her up.

"This is ridiculous. We need to dump her."

"I'm going through her pockets. We've got to find out something about her." Natasha reaches into Mickey's front right pocket and pulls out a single house key and a driver's license. "Jesus. She's just eighteen. Her name is Yvette. She lives in Cedarglen."

Hetty shrugs. "South?"

Natasha studies the address again. "Yeah, southwest." Natasha digs in her other pockets and comes up empty. "If she was carrying cash or a card, it's gone."

"My life with Evan is killing me."

"It's been killing you for years."

"I know. Help me?"

"You don't mean it."

"I know. I blame my younger self for this isolation."

Natasha can't read her friend's flushed, freckled face.

"Forget it, I'm good." Hetty stabilizes herself. "Let's take our little Mickey and get out of here. I'm ready."

| The table sits empty when the women walk past. Just the evidence of a good meal and drinks remain. At three other tables sit diners, noisy and consuming. Tyler and Evan wait at the door.

"Evan got the bill."

"Consider it my contribution to the arts." He puts his arm around Natasha. "What are we going to do with our young friend?"

"I'll drive her home."

"But the night is still young. Bring her to my place. We'll open some bourbon and sit on my grass."

"I'll come. After." She dangles the single house key. "I know where she lives now. Let me dump her. Then, I'll drink."

"Okay. So the party is still on?"

"Yes, I'll drive her home. You'll catch a cab with the others. I'll meet you. Good?"

"Oh, there's a horrible cloud of effort hanging over this. Just come over. We'll be up." Hetty texts while she speaks. Tyler holds open the door.

"Find us on my patch," Evan yells, his arm around Hetty. From behind, the two look young and carefree heading down the street, jackets pulled tightly closed against the summer wind, arms hooked for support against the evening's consumption, but Natasha knows it's more than that. They depend on each other and the life they've created.

"This way to my car."

And Tyler, with arm around Yvette's waist, follows Natasha across the street to the parking lot lit by the soft summer night's light.

| Natasha sits a quiet moment behind the wheel of her car with the window cracked a couple of centimetres. Mickey-Yvette is buckled in the back seat, head resting at an uncomfortable angle against the window, and Tyler is finishing a cigarette out on the sidewalk. Natasha's car smells musty; dank festering yeast from the body in the backseat. She is happy Tyler volunteered to drive with her, too happy, she knows, but her past runs long and deep with this man, and she can't help but enjoy this once yearly dinner together and the occasional series of texts that make her forget her age and remember what is what like to be desired. Tomorrow is another day and she can wrap herself back into her self-

doubting cloak then. The night has turned cool as Calgary summer nights do, but she needs the window open for the air. For her breath.

She sees Tyler's image in her mirror as he takes his final drag, drops the remnants of the cigarette and crushes it with his shoe. He opens the door and she puts the car in Drive before his seatbelt clicks shut. He pulls out his phone and asks her where Yvette's driver's license is. After plugging in the address, he tells Natasha the first street to be on the lookout for, before resting his head back on the headrest. He's functioning efficiently considering he's drunk. She's functioning well considering what happened between the two of them only six months ago.

"It's good of you to do this," he says to Natasha but his eyes are closed. Natasha looks in her rear-view mirror at the slumped and now familiar shape in her back seat.

"Goodness has nothing to do with it. Sobriety does."

Tyler laughs. "It's good to see you. Evan and Hetty, too. We'll go back?"

"We'll go back."

"Did you get that government job?"

"Nah."

"Sorry, Tash."

"It's all right. I missed the deadline by about two decades. So I went into the catering business with my sisters."

Tyler shifts in his seat, folds his arms.

"You must hate it."

"I do."

"So how do you get by?"

"With my obsession."

"Still me?"

She holds her breath. They both know it to be true. "Can't anymore. Gave up my phone."

"Ah."

"So, I took up books."

"Books are good."

"Yeah, they are. But, confession?"

"Hmm?"

"I smell them more than I read them."

"Oh, Tash."

Natasha looks Tyler's way but Tyler's eyes are closed, his face relaxed, peaceful. She takes his phone from his lap and follows the map.

| Stopping in front of a simple, stuccoed home at the curve of a cul-de-sac, Natasha leans in towards Tyler. His smell is warm and palatable, and she wishes she had held on to some youthful nerve to make him be accountable to what he said he might do to her via text. But she doesn't, so he won't. When they texted, she was safe behind her screen and she knows he was, too. Tyler smells of their night. She can smell the wine on his breath, the garlic and his last cigarette. She can also smell his shirt, the detergent he washed it in and the lotion he uses on his skin. Her favourite book, *The Buddha of Suburbia*, by Hanif Kureishi, smells like melting candle wax and oregano. Her favourite man, always and now, smells of a night out with friends. She whispers in Tyler's ear, "C'mon. Let's get rid of the kid."

| "Do you think we should have taken her to the hospital? Called the police?" Tyler lights a cigarette and leans against the car. This time Natasha joins him. He passes her the cigarette and she inhales.

"Hmph. You think?" They both look up the winding path and to the door they had just locked from the inside and closed after shoving Yvette in.

"Kind of late now."

"Evan's?"

"Sure."

"Who names their kid Moppy?"

"Hetty. You ask that every time."

"True. What a pair. You're coming too, right? Not disappearing home to your stack of sniffable books?"

"You're coming, too, not disappearing home to your wife?"

Tyler looks long and hard at Natasha. "I'm coming." He takes another drag and offers it back. Natasha declines. "Want me to drive?"

"Yes. But I've got it this time."

"Suppose so. But next time, I'll drive." Tyler looks at the burning end of his cigarette, takes two final quick puffs and flicks the butt into an empty flower bed.

"Sure."

"To Evan's and his fucking patch of grass."

Tyler settles into the seat, his knees high into the dashboard. And after driving a few moments and getting her bearings, Natasha takes her eyes off the road to look his way and breathe in his presence in her car. Just his presence. Not Yvette's, not Ted's, not Tyler's wife. Just Tyler's, as the late-night lights illuminate the two of them. Natasha feels happy. Even now, she'd prefer to have Tyler close to her and married than be back with Ted and married. With Tyler she is ageless and desirable.

Natasha slackens her stomach muscles as she turns north on Crowchild Trail towards Mount Royal and the patch of grass that brings Evan much joy, that will bring her and Tyler joy for a few more hours.

After, she will take a cab home.

One More Minute

JOAN CRATE

In the hill behind the house
flakes of mica dazzle the wind:
primordial magma hardened
to centuries of stars falling
through earth. Tonight

under a bolt of blue silk worn
here and there by chafe and mending
I'll wear stone and silver, a dress of moss
and barnacles. I'll adorn my tongue
with jewels and heavy metals,

try to sing.

You will hold me, take me over
the forest floor, our bodies locked
in a future of prolonged shadows
so much less remarkable than
the buried howls from a cat

caged alive with the corpse of its owner
in an ancient pyramid of Egypt
or the stain of a man rendered
on the steps of a bank in Hiroshima
         Oh God Oh God

let's dance and trip scream and sing like everything
is all right, like you're not sick, like nothing
is wrong at all. Torn open to the elements
we revel in the raw meat of our bodies.
Burning

         we turn
inside out light illuminating
lungs, livers, our hearts for a minute.

Just give us a few more fucking minutes.

The Shave

RONA ALTROWS

AFTER PAUL'S FUNERAL Amanda decided to shave off what was left of her pubic hair. Already some strands had greyed, some had gone brittle, bald patches had shown up. Enough.

In his own way, David Attenborough encouraged her to go ahead with the shave. Attenborough always calmed her. His voice, gravelly yet kind, that spoke of a long lifetime of observation, wonderment, continuous gathering of knowledge of the natural world. The way he pronounced glacier *glass-yer*. The way he made creatures of the tundra, the desert, the circumpolar boreal forest seem human or better, as they lived out their stories of lucky flukes, sacrifices for their young, fatal mistakes.

During this period of what was supposed to be grief, but actually was limbo, marked by a numbness she didn't mind as a temporary state, since it buffered her from unwanted intrusions, she watched an Attenborough special on oceans. King penguins waddled across her screen and plunked themselves down on hard ground, trapped in the torment of a growing itch. Amanda watched a penguin peck at itself relentlessly, until it had removed every feather in each of its four layers— the outer oily layer and the three layers of down—and in plucking off the feathers, the king penguin got rid of thousands of parasites picked up during its hunting forays at sea. This, Attenborough explained, was called the catastrophic moult.

Amanda felt an immediate affinity with the naked bird.

The king penguin stood exposed and vulnerable to predators, starving, surviving only on body fat, until every feather was replaced. Then, restored to its full capacity and power, it could again live fully.

| Amanda had never before given herself a pubic shave and was unsure what instrument would be optimal. A specially designed razor? All she had was a Gillette Venus, still pristine in its packaging, although she had bought it months earlier. She had intended to use the razor the next time she shaved her underarms, something she hardly had to do any more, that was how slowly the hairs grew. It was the same for her leg hairs. She had forgotten all about the Venus until this moment. Possibly, in using it, she would not be following best practices.

But it was what she had and it would have to do.

She had been shaved by a nurse thirty years before, while in labour with Sophie. Although Amanda's hypersensitive skin had not been cut, she had developed an excoriated rash, which she attributed to the hospital's chemically scented shaving cream.

This time she would go with aloe vera.

She decided to soak in the tub, get the area loosened up before moving in with the razor. A bath on the maternity ward would have been divine three decades back—although she had read recently that bathing slowed labour, so perhaps not. At the very least, she would have appreciated low lighting, as she had learned about in her prenatal classes, which Paul had rarely attended with her. What was the name of that French obstetrician they had taught her and her pregnant classmates about, the one who promoted gentle birthing methods? Le Something. Le Corbusier? No, that was an architect. Lesage? Politician.

However. Back to the shave. It was not as tricky as she had anticipated. True, she did not work with the panache of the king penguin, but she was careful and thorough. She tried using a makeup mirror but could not get the angles right, abandoned it, continued by feel alone. A rinse left the skin soft, pores happy. And no nicks.

| What did the shave mean? Amanda was not sure. She regretted not having read Jung.

She wanted to talk to Sophie about the shave but decided against it. Since Paul's final illness, Sophie had been extraordinarily protective of her. Maybe it was too early in Amanda's life for this to be happening. After all, she was in fairly good condition for a woman in her sixties. She did not need to be mothered by her daughter, at least not yet. Still, she let Sophie hug her a lot, and call her every day to check in, make sure she ate. She would not thwart Sophie's oversolicitousness for now, since it seemed to be part of what her daughter needed as she processed her father's death. Amanda knew instinctively that if she told Sophie about the shave, her daughter would find a way to turn it into a problem, the sign of a sinister turn in her mother's mental health.

But still, she was sorely tempted to share news of the shave with Sophie. Because Sophie *had* read Jung.

| She had never been able to convince Paul to scale back on creature comforts. He had insisted on so-called fine dining, revelled in receiving sycophantic service, while Amanda

worried that the servers were burning themselves. How could they not, with a hot platter poised gracefully over their lower arm while Paul slowly weighed the pros and cons of accepting the platter's contents. How many times had Amanda surreptitiously left large cash tips to restaurant and hotel staff, to assuage her guilt, make her feel less entangled in Paul's behaviour.

| Now, with Paul gone, she could live as she wished. She decided to mark the end of the ostentatiously rich part of her life by indulging in a final luxury, one she had not allowed herself but had secretly desired. Despite her misgivings, her fear of being misunderstood as a vacuous woman of privilege, she booked an appointment for a full body massage.

On the day, she walked past the elevator and up the stairs to the fifth-floor spa.

The aesthetician, Raylene, was kind, taking meticulous care even before she got started. Would Amanda prefer a soft or a firm touch? How firm? Raylene massaged all of her, even her breasts. Amanda was afraid she would feel invaded, but she did not. Instead, soothed. To her surprise, the scented oil did not irritate her skin. Maybe Raylene had gently extracted the oil from a king penguin's uropygial gland. Surely that was non-allergenic.

| She sold the house, rented a well-lit but spartan one-bedroom apartment, donated all her gowns to a small theatre company. Although not a worshipper of any kind, she liked the example set by the Buddha, how he had divested of all that was not necessary to his existence on any given day. How he had even refused offers of simple food for the following day. Today was all, today was enough.

As a young woman, she had been convinced she was the reincarnation of a medieval monk, and though she no longer believed this, she was still attracted to all forms of asceticism and their various expressions.

Friends worried. They told her they understood she was getting rid of everything out of grief for Paul, but perhaps she should not be so precipitous. In reality, they understood nothing. She and Paul had only maintained a facade of closeness. The truth was, they had not connected properly for years and had finally decided to end it, but before they'd been able to set a divorce in motion, pow—the diagnosis of stage three multiple myeloma. The doctors gave Paul the stark facts.

She and Paul reconciled enough to make life less brutal for him in his final stretch, which had turned out to be just under two years. She was by his side for every treatment, every appointment, every trip to Emergency.

Now she wondered if they'd made the right decision. Maybe it would have been better to live out the truth of their situation, to separate, to have Paul rely more on paid help for the practicalities of life—and for family support, Sophie. But Sophie and her partner Elissa had been going through a rough patch as a couple at that time, and Amanda hadn't wanted for Sophie to also be faced with meeting the day-to-day needs of her dying father.

So Amanda had seen Paul through his illness right to the end. He had appreciated her staying, or at least she thought so, although with him it was always hard to tell, which was one of the reasons she had wanted to leave him in the first place.

| Throughout their marriage she had known of his infidelities—he was sloppy at covering his tracks—but she had felt that with the dubious past she herself had brought into the marriage, she did not have solid grounds to complain.

| To see her way forward she felt she must first look back, right back to the days of Kevin, her on-and-off boyfriend for seven years. *L'amour de sa vie*, the French would call Kevin, the great passion of her life, who had, through his flagrant cheating, destroyed her ability to link sex with love. As a response, she cheated, too. Yet they kept getting back together. The one smart thing she had done with Kevin was not marry him.

But she had some excellent male friends. She tried not to have sex with them because in the few cases where she had done that, the friendship suffered. A person could not unsleep with a friend, as useful as that would have been.

Considering that she was an arts major, she surprised herself by socializing mainly with medical students. She thought of herself in those days as a doctor *manquée*. When her med-student friends showed her their thick, illustrated textbooks, she was awestruck. Although she considered herself a good memorizer, she knew she could never carry that skill far enough to get through the pounding medical school program. External intercostals, tunica intima, corniculate cartilage...how did her almost-doctor friends retain those terms in their minds? And remember what they meant?

One time, her friend Michael Borden, then in second year Medicine, snuck her into the anatomy lab. Was she alone among humans in adoring the smell of formaldehyde? Would this not have stood her in good stead if she'd had the brains to become, say, a coroner? Michael showed her the desiccated cadavers on gurneys. And heads, yes whole human heads, pickling in head-sized jars. Two big wooden boxes painted white. One labelled in red, ARMS. The other, LEGS. She peered into the ARMS one, and there they were, a collection of dried-out human arms with hands attached, all stuffed into the box willy-nilly, like toys. Yet the people who had once had those limbs attached to their bodies were, in death, teaching her friends about anterior meniscofemoral and deep transverse metacarpal ligaments. Those dead people were, through their disembodied limbs and severed heads, doing social good every day.

Michael himself now did social good every day, as a world-renowned epidemiologist. She'd see him on the television news from time to time, discussing whatever infectious disease was posing a threat in a certain region of the world that year.

| If only she had kept in touch with Michael Borden and her other university friends, if only she had followed her desire to enter politics and help transform the world, if only she had not squandered time with Kevin and even more time with Paul.

Well. At least Paul had fathered Sophie. Sophie was a treasure.

| In the days that followed she took solo hikes in the mountains, and as she walked the trails, she speculated on what a relationship would be like with a new lover, someone brilliant and gentle yet spunky, someone who could make her laugh. She began to feel wistful for an era in which she had not lived, when she might have discreetly pursued a countertenor, a castrato with a sparkling soul and a generous heart. Her vaginal dryness and wall-thinning would mean nothing to him, or to her. Every night he would sing her to sleep.

But no. Escape would not do. Not anymore.

Leboyer! That was the French doctor's name. Revolutionary ideas. Frequently misunderstood. She felt for him.

Feeling. It was back. All she'd ever wanted was to love, be loved, do social good every day. A way would present itself, and soon. She felt it.

Her pubic hair had grown back, all white. Amanda liked it.

TIMELINES

Telescoping

JULIE SEDIVY

I'M AWESTRUCK by the woman who used to occupy my body. She'd be up long before dawn preparing her university lectures for the coming day, then she'd shake the kids out of bed like ripe apples, feed them breakfast, escort them to school, and settle in for a day of teaching, faculty meetings, lab meetings, meetings with graduate students, meetings with research collaborators...and in the cracks and crevices between meetings and classes, she'd send emails, fill out reports, read an article or two, complete reviews, write an abstract to submit to an upcoming conference, plot out a grant proposal. Later she'd pick up the younger child from daycare, make dinner while doling out advice about home-work and strained friendships and the injustice of teachers, read a bedtime chapter or two from Harry Potter or Terry Pratchett, then spend the quiet evening hours writing. Where was the fuel for all this activity? When I look back in time, I see a woman ravenous for expansion. The world was large and she wanted to pour herself into as much of its space as possible, to absorb as much of it into herself as she could. The more she craved was distilled to a desire potent enough to power her, on its fumes alone, through each crammed, exhausting, productive day.

I can no longer live my days like that. And I can't blame it all on dwindling energy, the struggle to get a full night's sleep under the tyranny of perimenopausal insomnia, or the ever-increasing number of hours needed just to keep my body running smoothly. It's true that between visits to the doctor or physiotherapist and a devoutly observed gym schedule, I feel like a vintage vehicle that needs constant maintenance—and still spends an inordinate amount of time in the shop. But there's something else behind my wilting ambition. It's that more and more, I feel the lure of small things, things that pull me from the far edges of my desires, tamp down my seeking self, and anchor me to the luminous here and now. More and more, I'm drawn to the pleasure of a long dinner spent in conversation. There is a book I need to write, but I let the evening hours slip by listening to birdsong and watching the shifting sunlight amble its way through my garden while I sip a glass of wine, mesmerized by the way the light strikes the red liquid in my glass and sprays its energy in all directions. A phone call with my sister sprawls out over two languid hours, in discussion of profoundly non-urgent matters such as the books we've recently read or alternative careers we fantasize about. I take a morning walk in the woods, and the violets that have just released their blooms seem more absorbing than the work I left on my desk. My younger self was willing to sacrifice such pleasures. But lately I find I am not.

| I learn that I'm not alone in feeling the growing tug of everyday pleasures as I get older, or in allowing myself to be seduced by them. Laura Carstensen, a psychologist who has spent her life studying people's goals and priorities, has found

that as we age, we devote more care to what feels meaningful or satisfying in the present. Our attention is reeled in from far-off horizons. There is less exploring, more tending. When Carstensen asks her subjects if they would rather spend time with a close relative or an interesting new friend, she finds that younger people are keen to expand their social network; older people are drawn to the warmth of deeper personal bonds. Younger people eagerly throw their energies after nebulous rewards in the future; they want to learn new skills, seek new experiences, stockpile new achievements. With age, apparently, we become more accomplished practitioners of Zen. We rage less, strive less, want less.

And by all accounts, this makes us happier. Carstensen has found that even as their world shrinks in scope, old people often insist they are more content than ever. The outrageous losses of old age are miraculously dwarfed by the pleasures offered up by each moment, pleasures that may not even be visible to anyone else. I am reminded of the account given by writer Sharon Butala in her book *Where I Live Now* of her mother in the last days before her death from breast cancer. Butala asked her mother, weak and bedridden and about to succumb to a coma from which she'd never awaken, to name the best time of her life. Expecting her mother to reminisce about the idyllic days of her youth or the period of burgeoning independence in her midlife years after her children were grown, Butala was stunned when her mother pointed a shaky hand down at her own chest for emphasis, and asserted "Now!"—in a voice so feeble it could barely be heard. And indeed, ruminates her daughter, it was toward the very end of the life of this "very smart woman," when her days contained little aside from gardening, reading historical novels, watching television, and visiting with a smattering of family members, that her mother had appeared the most calm and contented, the least angry and dissatisfied. "I think all of this," marvels Butala, "might have been a kind of happiness."

If such happiness is a form of wisdom, it's a wisdom that evidently does not need a lifetime of cultivation. It just needs limits. Carstensen argues that it's not age or even experience that shifts our focus to the present moment; rather, it's an awareness of the finiteness of time. In some of her work, she has asked young people to imagine they are afflicted with a terminal illness and then had them choose among various ways to spend their time. They choose as if they were much older. She has asked old people to imagine a new medical breakthrough that will add twenty years to their life. They choose as if they were much younger. When they are freed from time's limits, they abandon their Zenlike priorities and give space to hunger and wanting and the dissatisfactions these can bring. The pleasures of the moment suddenly lose their potency.

| I wish I could say that as I age, I am making a serene transition toward the wisdom of living more deeply in the moment. But rather than a gradual, gentle shifting of gaze, I find myself oscillating between priorities and perspectives. It's as if, at any given time, my vision flips between the short and the long end of a telescope. My eyes are either trained on the distance or on what is right in front of me. The wanting is still there, strong as ever, the siren song of more has not left me alone. But the small pleasures of the moment have become far more compelling, diluting my ambition. When I yield to them, these moments are imbued with an intense satisfaction, but I'm not sure I feel more content overall. I feel the clash of conflicting urges more often, constantly second-guessing myself: which lens should I be looking

through right now? I'm like an Alice in Wonderland, shutting up like a telescope, delighted to enter the smaller doors into new gardens, but then suddenly finding myself blown up in size. I never know how much space to occupy.

Is my conflict sharpened by the fact of being female? As a woman, I have so often been plunged into ambivalence over my ambition. It's hard not to be suspicious of any impulse that dampens the urge to achieve—is this impulse my own, or have I been infected by society's discomfort with ambitious women?

I once read an essay by David Brooks, a columnist for *The New York Times*, in which he sang the praises of "a small, happy life." He wrote about people who had found contentment by unhitching themselves from aspiration and devoting their lives to modest actions of kindness and connection. A part of me felt a sense of relief upon reading this, a gratitude for the assurance that I was right to want to turn my gaze away from the broad horizon. But another part—the female part that has so often been nudged to moderate her desires—bristled. Why was this assurance being offered by a person who claimed a large space for himself in the large world, a person who himself had not and was unlikely to choose to live a small life, no matter how happy? Easy for you to say, I thought, when you have always had the license to spread your ambition over the world. Is this just your privilege-guilt talking, when you soothe the rest of us with the runner-up prize of a small, happy life?

Even my dreams reveal my confusion about which lens to look through. For several years now, I've had recurring dreams in which I discover I have a fatal illness. In one of these dreams, I learn I have a mere two days left to live. Just as I feel my dream-mind grasp this fact, settling on how best to spend these precious two days, I wake up to the realization that I might have much more time than that. I likely have at least two months, my waking mind realizes in wonder, or even two years, or even twenty years. I might even have another forty. Time swells to luxurious proportions. My aspirations billow.

| My dream-mind had it wrong all along. It's not my longevity but my husband's that is in serious question; he has oral cancer, a three-centimetre tumour nestled in his tongue and tonsils. He also has a tumour, probably cancerous, on his solitary kidney, which is about to be blasted with chemotherapy to help shrink the cancer in his mouth. The chemotherapy won't shrink the kidney cancer—that will require surgery—but it may damage his one blighted kidney.

There are times when patterns begin to seem prophetic, and the pattern I can't stop thinking about is the string of lengthy widowhoods that runs through my family. The men in my family are prone to dropping dead, the women live on and on. One of my grandmothers was widowed for more than five decades, the other for almost four, despite her conviction that she would be joining her husband soon after his death. My aunt's husband died with no warning in his fifties, leaving her to soldier on for another half-lifetime. My father died in his sleep years ago; my mother, I am sure, will live to be a hundred. How can I have failed to warn my husband of the hazards he incurred by entering into our family?

Suddenly, we are looking through the short end of the telescope every day. In his book *The Emperor of All Maladies*, physician Siddhartha Mukherjee writes that the experience of undergoing cancer treatment is like being in a concentration camp—the world outside fades away and ceases to exist for the patient and his family. The future is erased. Life exists only within the prison walls.

However, the constraints of a prison can—precisely because of this distortion of vision—cajole beauty from whatever is at hand. Several years ago, I had a serious vestibular disorder that restricted my mobility and shrank my own world. Driving was impossible. Walking even a block left me gasping with nausea, and the sensory overload of a pub or a coffee shop kept me from seeing friends, even if I had been able travel to these places. It was early summertime, a time when I would normally spend long days hiking in the mountains, taking in panoramic views, or climbing steep rock faces with my husband. I tried to imagine a life limited to my house and yard. I went out and bought a good camera and a macro lens and found I could spend hours lying on my stomach, trying to capture the elegant tension of a fern as it prepared to unclench its greenness, or finding the precise angle at which one could see the razor-line edge of a single rose petal set off against its sea of velvet pink. I no longer dwelled on the prospect of never again being able to scale a peak or walk along a mountain ridge or enjoy the thrum of urban life. There was a lifetime's worth of tiny things in my garden that had yet to be explored.

As my husband progresses through his daily regimen of chemotherapy and radiation, our lens becomes a macro lens, tightly focused on this minute, as any segments of time beyond that blur entirely out of focus. There is this moment of him weaving in and out of a light doze as his veins accept the drip of anti-nausea medication; he occasionally becomes lucid enough to become aware of my presence while I sit next to him and work my way through the stack of pages I am proofreading, his awareness signaled less by a smile than a slight relaxation of his face. There is this moment as we assemble a jigsaw puzzle, waiting for him to be called into the radiation room where he will have his masked head bolted down to the table to offer a steady target for the external beam's assault. Our hands nuzzle each other as we finger the small pieces, moving them here and there on the table, and the rhythm of his breathing seeps into my own body, colonizes my heartbeat. Incredibly, I think, these moments are enough. There may never be another morning sweetened by our lovemaking, or a trail pounded out by our feet in lockstep, or a trip taken with our children. But these moments, incredibly, feel like enough. They can't obliterate the vomiting, the opiate disorientation, the ropes of phlegm in his throat, the discomfort of the feeding tube threaded through his nose down to his stomach, or anything else about the sheer misery that is oral cancer and its treatment. But under the macro lens, these most ordinary of moments, normally so insignificant as to be passed over on our way to other more important, more vivid, more urgent experiences, instill reverence. It is as Mary Oliver has said: attention is the beginning of devotion. And attention, it seems, is best cultivated under constraint. Attention is a gift bestowed by mortality.

| But how quickly we discard these gifts when we are given the opportunity to shuck constraints and turn a blind eye to mortality. Three months after my husband's treatment ends, scans of his body reveal that his oral cancer has melted away, leaving no discernible trace. It takes me no more than a month—much less time than it takes him, who still has to inhabit a body wrecked by treatment—for my vision to shift. I ease into the presuppositions that undergird most of the days of our lives. I presuppose that he will be alive next month and next year and, most likely, ten years after that. I presuppose longevity like I presuppose that the lights will come on if I flick the switch and that grocery-store shelves

will be stocked with food. The world outside of cancer's prison begins to unblur.

I become aware of the editor waiting for a manuscript, of the discoveries my colleagues have made and the books my friends have launched while I sat in hospital rooms. I am restless, feeling hemmed in by caregiving, worn down by the dreariness of disease, craving freedom, resentful of how cramped my intellectual muscles have become. My perception of time and space is suddenly out of sync with my husband's, as if I have jumped into a new timeline but keep colliding with the old. He is still in the throes of recovery. For him, time still moves at the speed of single breaths. His major daily accomplishments include learning to swallow oatmeal.

I've become preoccupied by another pattern: I read a study that found that men are six times more likely to abandon a wife with a life-threatening illness than the other way around. When a woman is diagnosed with cancer, her risk of divorce is far greater than that of a woman in the general population; for men, cancer seems to be a protective measure against divorce, binding their wives to them more securely.

I can imagine several reasons for this. But most of all, I wonder whether men have a harder time tolerating the constraints of a timeline that is imposed on them by another body—a body they can still flee, along with its small life. Perhaps they are freed by a choice that few women feel they have. Perhaps, granted that choice, men are deprived of a devotional state of heightened attention.

| It occurs to me that our presuppositions of longevity, which define the "normal" outlines of a life, are in fact deeply abnormal. Most humans, at most times and in most places, did not have the luxury of a "normal" lifespan of some eighty-odd years. What was life like for these swaths of humanity

who lived without presupposition? Were the colours of the sky more vivid, the after-scent of a rainstorm more invigorating? Was it easier to live a small, happy life? Is mindfulness a prescription that only modern humans require?

There is an app you can download onto your phone that will remind you of your mortality throughout your day. The website for the *WeCroak* app says that it is "inspired by a Bhutanese folk saying: to be a happy person, one must contemplate death five times daily." Each day, the app will deliver "five invitations to stop and think about death. Our invitations come at random times and at any moment, just like death." When prompted, the user can open the app and read a poetic or thoughtful quote about death.

What was life like, I wonder, when you needed no "invitations" to think about death, had no reasonable way to calculate your probable lifespan, when mortality could announce itself at any time, not by an app, but by a ruptured placenta during childbirth, the infection from a small cut celebrating a victory over your bloodstream, a grass fire blazing out of control in your village, tuberculosis cozying up to your lungs?

As youth recedes farther and farther behind me, perhaps I'm getting closer to this more natural way of living. I still seek comfort in statistics, but there is always a part of me that knows—whether waking or dreaming—that death now walks in the same spaces I do, brushing against the hem of my skirt or touching the clothing of someone I love. I would no longer be shocked to find death standing stock still in the middle of my path. It could assert its presence at any time, in a swift stroke, as a sudden embolism, at the next doctor's appointment.

In the meantime: breathe in the fragrance of a child's hair. Open your pores to the morning breeze. Study the slope of your beloved's cheek. All of this may soon be gone.

Rajiana

MONI BRAR

this village was her second home.
winter mornings with fog
so thick
you could cup it with your heart.
the whirring of peacocks on the rooftop,
iridescent feathers left behind,
small gifts
for the children to find.
the rustle of mourning doves
at daybreak.

the ping of metal, the first drop
smooth and heavy as a swollen belly.
water buffalo milk hits the pail soon
to be transformed into
    cha
    butter
    lassi
    nighttime bedside warm milk
to make eyelids heavy.

crisp cotton branches
snap, feed, crackle in
the eager mouth of the *chulha*,
ebbing the chill,
fueling the day.
plumes of smoke rise,
turning
thin as a young girl's wrist,
blackening the *rasoi*,
its shelves bare.

she lies on a *munjaa*,
the cot
women who came before her wove.
their hands long gone
their bodies and its fibres
frayed
loose ends blown away.
her limbs are limp, greedy
for memories, of hers and others.

she came to Rajiana
with rapture in her eyes
and a nose ring.
a young bride
filled with hope as sweet as
marigolds.
now, something dank
spools from her belly,
unbidden, unkept
it ages her body, soul.

like a soothing ritual
she breathes out.
she prays in whispers
for strength or release.
the only thing growing is
her darkness,
nourished and blinding.
Rajiana was never home.

chulha: a traditional small earthen or brick stove built on
    the ground
rasoi: kitchen
munjaa: a traditional woven bed used across the Indian
    subcontinent. It is a single cot made from cotton, natural
    fibres, and date leaves.

Aging in Three-Year Increments

LAURA WERSHLER

I TAKE A DEEP BREATH, roll back my shoulders, tighten
every muscle, and extend my spine upwards. As I visualize
the spaces between my vertebrae expanding, I feel the pressure of the height-measuring bar pushing down on my head.
Am I shorter today than I was three years ago?

As a participant in the Canadian Longitudinal Study on
Aging (CLSA), I am attending my third round of testing at
the data-collection site in Calgary, one of eleven across the
country. Between 2010 and 2015, more than 50,000 men and
women between the ages of forty-five and eighty-five were
recruited for this national, long-term study to determine the
impact of both medical and non-medical factors contributing
to aging. When the study ends in 2033, I'll either be eighty or
dead.

Several weeks ago, I hosted a research assistant for the
in-home interview, during which my eating habits, exercise activities, medical history, medication usage, family and
social relationships, transportation needs and means, mental
wellness, and community engagement were documented.
This morning, May 7, 2019, I arrived ready to be poked,
prodded, scanned, and interrogated, again. Ready to do my

part to help science understand the factors that contribute to healthy aging. But right here, right now, all I care about is how *I* am aging. Am I shorter or weaker than I was three years ago? Will my test performance demonstrate a decline in physical mobility? A degradation of my cognitive function? Am I using it or losing it?

I know I look good for my age. At least that's what many people tell me. But at sixty-five, I've come to understand that what matters most is not how I look, but how I move, how I think, how I feel. Aches and pains and hearing aids aside, I'm feeling strong and wise and connected.

Self-rated physical and psychological health is part of the study's data collection. We already know, from a published report on CLSA baseline data collected from 2010–2015, that 90 per cent of Canadians aged forty-five to eighty-five rated their general health as good, very good, or excellent. Perhaps healthy older adults were more likely to accept the randomly generated requests to join the study. Or maybe some of us are deluding ourselves.

Today's data collection starts with a physical assessment by Research Assistant Number One. First, the basics: blood pressure, height, weight, and body mass index. Spirometry to determine lung capacity. Electrocardiogram to evaluate heart function. Carotid intima-media thickness test, or CIMT, to measure the thickness of the inner two layers of my carotid artery. Even subtle changes in arterial thickness can put me at risk for heart disease and stroke. This is the study participant's bonus. If research assistants find indicators of ill health, on tests one might not expect to receive during routine medical check-ups, we will be alerted to see our primary-care physicians for follow-up. I'm assured my test result shows no evidence of atherosclerosis. My carotid artery gets another A–.

The bone density scan, conducted by Research Assistant Number Two, will produce a FRAX score that will appear on the printed two-page report handed to me before I leave today. The Fracture Risk Assessment Tool tells me the risk of suffering a major fracture, due to diminished bone density, over the next ten years. Three years ago, it was considered low, a less than 10 per cent chance of breaking my hip, spine, wrist, or shoulder should I slip and fall on Calgary's icy winter streets.

Aging women often worry about their bones because modern medicine has done such an awesome job of pathologizing what is normal about women's bodies. Such as losing a percentage of our bone density post-menopause. For most of us, the best way to avoid fractures will be to avoid falls. The best way to avoid falls is to maintain core muscle strength, flexibility, and balance control. My all-female gym is full of older women training hard to do so. The place may be called Spa Lady, but it is no day at the spa: our skin glows because we sweat. We don't work out to defy our ages. We lift iron, practice yoga, and take cardio classes to trash the stereotype of the frail older woman.

When the memory and cognitive tests begin, I'm itching to prove I'm as sharp as I was in 2016, or that any decline I may demonstrate is occurring at a glacial pace. Wait—think climate change—new metaphor required.

Before the first test, I am told that at some random time during the session an alarm will sound. When I hear it, I am to take from the padded envelope Research Assistant Number Two now shows me, emptying its contents to reveal various bills and coins, the five-dollar bill to give to her and the ten-dollar bill to keep for myself. I repeat the instructions back to her before a card with coloured dots is thrust into my hand.

I am asked to say the colour of the dots printed like a grid across the page. I "read" from left to right until I come to the end of about six or eight rows. Green, red, yellow, blue; yellow, red, blue, green. The next card has words instead of dots. Blue, red, yellow, and green are printed out, but the colours and words don't match. I'm to "read" colour. If the word blue is printed in yellow, the right answer is yellow. I read from left to right, at a slightly slower pace than I read the dots, careful to let the colour register before the word. The third card has simple words printed in the four colours. I read this card at an even slower, step-by-step pace, and make at least one mistake I am aware of. It's a kind of cognitive multitasking, something I try to do only when the stakes are low. Such as setting up the ironing board behind the couch to watch *The National* while I steam my summer linens.

Next, a word game. I am asked to name as many words as possible that start with the letter A. The words must be unique, not related like ask, asked, asking. I have three chances to make an impression with my vocabulary and can tell I am warming up as the test advances. On F, I say the words "fairy" and "ferry." I think of stopping to explain I was not repeating a word, but don't; I have only sixty seconds to spill as many words as I can think of. On s, I shift to an association technique—sand, sea, sky, stars, shining, sunshine—reducing the time I wasted struggling to think of distinct words on A and F. I wonder, what does this test demonstrate? I wonder, what will it do for my brain if I make it a daily practice? I tell myself to remember to practice this task in advance of my data-collection visit in 2022. Can you game aging?

The alarm rings in the middle of a long series of questions that appear to be testing my powers of recall. I stop in mid-answer, pick up the envelope, fish out the fiver to hand to the research assistant, and take the ten-dollar bill for myself. "Do I get to keep it?" I ask. She smiles and reaches for the bill. It's not about the money, it's about my memory.

If she'd asked me to name twenty people I know by first and last name, I might have failed miserably today. These past few weeks, people's last names have been escaping me. Friends, celebrities, politicians. A week ago, I was in a book store wanting to buy the recently published book by a young writer I've come to know. I couldn't for the life of me recall her last name or the title of her book, but then an aid to daily living came to my rescue. I opened Twitter on my phone and searched her first name, the uniquely spelled Nikki. Up popped her Twitter handle @nikkireimer and, once a staff member pointed me to the poetry shelves, I found *My Heart is a Rose Manhattan*.

My heart loves the idea that "aids to daily living" go far beyond services and products to assist those with long-term disabilities or chronic and terminal illness. Ageism and ableism are associated with the phrase "aids to daily living," yet it can be applied to the way most of us live our lives. Who can deny that Twitter, Facebook, and Google are aids to daily modern living? These gladdening, maddening technologies connect us to friends, family, and colleagues, and to information that enhances our lives. People of all ages and stages use them. What about housekeepers and landscapers? Aids to daily living. Meal-kit companies and restaurant delivery services? Meals on Wheels for busy families or those who don't want, or know how, to cook—aids to daily eating.

If we acknowledge that everyone uses such aids to assist with the rigours of life, perhaps the kind of aids most associated with aging would be embraced more enthusiastically by those who need them. I wear my Unitron N Moxi Fit 800 hearing aids sixteen hours a day. (Without them I might not have heard that high-pitched alarm.) It's taken almost a thousand days to work the price per wearing of my everyday "luxury" accessory down to about $4.60 a day, or sixty-three cents an hour. But the difference this aid to daily living has made to my life is priceless.

Beyond the treasure trove of lost sounds I rediscovered upon getting hearing aids—the crackle of paper as I turn a page, the clash of cutlery against porcelain, the soft swish of a breeze through the trees outside my bedroom window—I am protecting myself against depression, dementia, social isolation, memory loss, falls, and even cardiovascular disease.

I believe my hearing aids prevent marital squabbles, the ones caused by miscommunication. I also owe my satisfying part-time job as a sales associate in a women's clothing shop to my hearing aids. I'd have quit or been kindly let go by now if I had not corrected my hearing impairment.

Getting hearing aids when I did was one of the best decisions I've ever made, right up there with saying sayonara to my identity as a brunette. I didn't need those super-expensive invisible aids I tried first, the ones that fit right inside my ear canal. Although no one notices my platinum-coloured hearing helpers nestled behind my ears, camouflaged by silver hair, I tell everyone I have them. I want everyone to know that not getting hearing aids when you need them speeds up aging.

I know I won't pass the hearing test today because the research assistant asks me to remove my aids. With my eyes squeezed shut to block out competing sensory information, I strain to hear the faint, distant beeps at varying frequencies so I might accurately push the sound indicator button with my right thumb. To no avail. The two-page report I'll be handed at the end of the session will confirm a four-frequency fail in both ears, the kind of hearing loss that affects the ability to comprehend speech.

My disengagement from conversations I couldn't follow in cars, restaurants, and noisy environments, and my rising discomfort with asking people to repeat themselves, is what prompted me to see an audiologist. According to a 2015 Statistics Canada report called "The Prevalence of Hearing Loss Among Canadians Aged 20–79," only 12 per cent of Canadian adults with a measured hearing loss use hearing aids. I hope the Canadian Longitudinal Study on Aging will amass enough evidence about the negative health consequences of untreated hearing loss to prompt nationwide policies that ensure no one goes without treatment. Hearing aids should not be, for anyone, an unaffordable luxury.

Up next are the strength tests. I've unknowingly been preparing for this since 1998 when I started weight-resistance training. I did it to feel strong and to stay fit, but it was hundreds of visits to the long-term care community where my mother lived for almost three years, from 2011 to 2014, that convinced me to keep doing it. I saw the consequences of functional disability every time I entered the facility. Many residents, mostly women over a wide age range, were there because they could not physically take care of themselves. I'm not suggesting they were responsible for their mobility issues—arthritis, diabetes, chronic pain take a heavy toll—but their physical challenges, including those of my ninety-five-year-old mother, motivated me to never stop pumping iron.

The first strength test seems simple. Research Assistant Number Three directs me to sit in a chair, stand up, walk to the green line taped on the floor twenty feet away, turn around, walk back, and sit down. He will time my round trip. How fast did I do this three years ago? I do not use my arms to push myself out of the chair or to ease my way back into the chair. My leg muscles do all the work. Loss of muscle mass and strength as we age was once thought inevitable, but a 2011 study published in *The Physicians and Sports Medicine* journal demonstrated unequivocally that it is not.

Study subjects were twenty male and twenty female recreational masters triathletes between the ages of forty and eighty-one who trained four to five times a week. Strength and fitness tests showed that neither leg-muscle size nor strength declined significantly with age. But it is the MRI photos comparing the quadricep muscles of forty- and seventy-year-old triathletes and a seventy-four-year-old sedentary man that shockingly illustrate the benefit of regular strength training. I've bookmarked the link to "chronic exercise preserves lean muscle mass-images" to remind myself to use them or lose them.

I'm no masters athlete and never will be, but I know the value of my twice-a-week Iron Reps class, all those squats with twenty-five pounds on my back, my hiking forays into Kananaskis Country and the Rocky Mountains, and my daily walks in Fish Creek Park behind my neighbourhood. I know, as the study concluded, that "maintenance of muscle mass and strength may decrease or eliminate the falls, functional decline, and loss of independence that are commonly seen in aging adults."

Good balance, all about leg and core strength, helps prevents falls. It follows that balance is measured for this study. I must stand on one bare foot, then the other, for as long as I can, up to sixty seconds. I rest the raised foot against my calf, the tree pose in yoga, focusing on a smudge on the wall, and hit the minute mark on both legs.

The next task is to stand up, walk forward a few steps, walk back and sit down, five times as fast as possible. I do this, again, without using my arms. Will I still be able to do so when I'm sixty-eight?

Last assessed is grip strength. My third attempt is decent, but, full disclosure, at my house jar-opening is now a two-person activity. What would I do if I lived alone?

The finish line is in sight when the vision testing begins. Like most people my age, I wear glasses. This morning the tiny screw holding arm to frame fell out. My husband did his best to screw it back in, but I can tell my lenses are not correctly aligned. This will affect my visual acuity score. Unlike the hearing test where they asked me to remove my hearing aids, I keep my glasses on for the vision test. I find this a contradiction. If they want to know how I see with my glasses on, shouldn't they want to know how I hear while wearing my aids? This suggests a key difference in the way visual aids and hearing aids are perceived on the continuum of aids to daily living.

Adjusting to glasses is supposed to be easier than adjusting to hearing aids. And it may be, at first. Put on glasses and you can see. Put in hearing aids and it may take weeks to find the right model and the right settings. But once those adjustments are made, hearing aids can be a breeze, compared to the annoyance of constantly adjusting one's visual field. I take my glasses on and off several times a day: off for the computer, one-on-one conversations, and reading; on for household tasks, watching TV, and outdoor activities. For work in the clothing shop, I wear just one contact lens, so that I can see customers' faces across the room and read the tiny print on the garment hangtags. My glasses cannot handle all my visual needs. And I can't even wear them when I need them most, for plucking my eyebrows and putting on makeup.

When I spent over two hundred dollars to buy a Simplehuman sensor mirror, with natural lighting and five-times magnification to view my face "with enhanced clarity and detail," I justified the expenditure as yet another aid for daily living. The sooner the better, I thought. Women may make jokes about our chin hairs but, for some of us, managing facial hair is serious business. Call it vanity if you must, but ageism will discriminate for the smallest of perceived indiscretions. Thank goodness the mirror's flattering circle of light also alerts me to sleep residue in the corners of my eyes and blueberry stains (left from a breakfast of steel-cut oats and berries) on the corners of my mouth, neither of which I can see in the bathroom mirror. The travel-size version of this brilliant technology is on my wish list.

In between reading the eye chart and diagnostic tests that shine light and blow air into your eyes, this third research assistant poses one more memory test and many more questions. This time I have to watch for an analogue clock, off to my left, to reach an appointed hour, then pull a square of laminated paper printed with the number 17 out of another envelope to hand him. I keep one eye on the clock and one eye on the assistant as he asks about my home and family life, my social support systems, my emotional well-being and mental health, and my sense of safety at home and in the community where I live. Questions about the social determinants of health we don't always think about when we think about aging. The kinds of questions that might elicit disclosures of serious depression, unsafe living conditions, loneliness, neglect, or abuse. When asked how often I feel as if I have no one to talk to when I have a problem or need support, it is with deep gratitude that I can answer, "Never."

The complexities of aging, as if woven into an intricate tapestry, cast a shadow over the exuberance I've felt for much of the morning. I know it's not all about me. I know how important this longitudinal study is to finding ways to help my fellow baby boomers and the generations to follow, live both long and well. With life expectancy soaring, and the prediction by Statistics Canada that by 2031 one in four Canadians will have surpassed the traditional retirement age of sixty-five, our need to understand healthy aging has never been more urgent.

As the lab technician draws over a dozen vials of my blood, on the last stop of the data collection circuit, I ponder how being a participant in this study has influenced my ideas and attitudes about aging. I certainly have a more holistic understanding of the myriad factors that influence aging outcomes. It's not just about diet, exercise, and the retention of one's senses and faculties, although these three-year reference points are powerful motivation to maintain healthy habits. I'd be letting my present and future self down if I didn't. But ultimately, my intimate relationships with family and friends are the vital link to my future well-being as an aging woman. It will be their love and kindness I depend upon should circumstances change, illness strike, or calamity befall.

Research Assistant Number Three, my favourite of the morning, is the one to hand me the two-page report on the measurements taken today. I scan the parameters laid out in neat, easy-to-read charts. Under the heading "Interpretation" the word "Normal" repeats down the columns. My bone fracture risk is still low. The Hearing Threshold chart documents my four-frequency failure to hear at 40 decibels, the sound level at which conversational speech is normally heard. My visual acuity score, 20/32 with correction, suggests it's time to get new glasses. When I get home, I will compare this report to my last and discover that I am 0.3 centimetres shorter than I was three years ago.

The inevitable shrinking woman? I think not.

Lilly's Funeral

MADELAINE SHAW-WONG

SHE'S GONE, passed away, deceased...the words reverberate
in my brain without meaning. A fog settled over me when
I heard the bad news and still hasn't lifted. I stand over her,
grasping the edges of the coffin, trying to work up the courage
to touch her. That's not Lilly, yet it is. Her skin resembles
molded clay instead of flesh. She looks inhuman, like a ghastly
mannequin, a Lilly facsimile. I press the palm of my hand
against my chest to ease the sharp pain, hope I'm not having
a heart attack.

Lilly's cheeks are tinted pink and her lips red, though she
rarely wore makeup when she was alive. The goal is to make
the deceased look more presentable, less...dead. Morticians
remove all the blood from bodies and pump them full of
embalming fluid in preparation for the viewing. That might
account for the puffiness of Lilly's face. Her eyes are shut,
giving the illusion of sleep. In the old days, undertakers put
pennies over the eyes. Now, they use eye caps to keep the lids
shut, better than staring into the lifeless eyes of the departed.
They also wire the jaws and glue the lips together, so the
mouth doesn't hang open. Lilly loved talking. I wonder what
she'd think of that.

Her head is on a pillow, to help her "rest in peace." Her hands are folded across her chest with a rosary looped between her hard, claw-like fingers. Those aren't the hands I remember. Her strong hands played piano. Her gentle hands cuddled children and held mine when I got my cancer diagnoses. I thought I'd be the first to go, but I beat the disease.

If I touch her maybe that will make it real and I can emerge from this haze. I reach down and place my hand on her cheek, but draw back, trembling. She's like ice. Naturally, they'd kept her in refrigeration since she passed four days ago.

A child comes to stand beside me, Lilly's five-year-old grandson. He stands on tiptoe and peers over the edge of the coffin. The straw-coloured hair on the back of his head is sticking up at odd angles, as if he's just gotten out of bed. Like me, he's not crying. He looks up at me with wide eyes and puts his small hand on my forearm. "My grandma was old, Dot. That's why she died."

I place my hand on the top of his head. "Yes. That's right."

She was just one year older than me. Sixty-four isn't old, but it isn't young, either. To a child it may seem like an impossibly large number. My stomach is rolling. Sweat prickles on my scalp. If she can suddenly die, then I...

| Her daughter, Carly, called me four days ago. "You better sit down, Dot," she said. Her voice was shaky and full of gravel.

I sat. My throat went dry. When someone tells you to sit down, it can't be good.

"My mom died this morning."

I clutched the front of my blouse and gasped. I was stunned, unable to breathe, like a punch in the stomach. The room swirled around me. I had just talked to Lilly the day before. She called to delay our lunch date, due to a bad cough.

"Dot? You there?"

When I could catch my breath, I said, "This can't be happening."

"She had a stroke."

I struggled to understand. "She said wasn't feeling well. I should have been there—"

"It was very fast, Dot. I went to check on her this morning when she didn't answer her phone."

Suddenly cold, I took the throw blanket off the back of the couch and wrapped it around my shoulders. "You're the one who found her, Carly?"

"The doctor said she probably passed a few hours before I arrived."

I didn't cry when I heard the news. I still haven't cried, though I loved her dearly. There's no explaining it.

| The time for viewing is finished, and we herd into the body of the church for the eulogies and mass. I sit beside Lilly's family and breathe slowly, in and out, in and out, struggling for self-control. I'm angry at Lilly for leaving me and I'm angry at God. How dare he take my friend away! Lilly was my rock. I thought she was invincible.

They asked me to offer a eulogy, but I refused. I can't adequately express the friendship we shared over the last forty-two years. Her cousin gets up and goes to the microphone. He tells us about Lilly's accomplishments and what a fine person she was. I don't disagree, but I notice that he doesn't mention Lilly's short temper or tendency to gossip.

I stare at the funeral card. The picture of Lilly is one that I took. She's smiling, sitting beneath a beach umbrella with the ocean in the background. We took a trip to Mexico a few years ago. I refused to wear a swimsuit, thinking I was too fat.

Carly puts her young hand on mine and squeezes. My hands used to be pretty like hers. Now they're covered with lines and liver-spots. Damn, I hate getting old. I put the card in my purse and arrange my blouse to cover my belly rolls.

| Paul left me for another woman, someone younger and thinner than me. I spent years, afterwards, fluctuating between joining Weight Watchers to drop forty pounds and the advice to "love the skin you're in." I came to accept the fact that I would spend the rest of my days as a single woman. No man will be interested in a chub like me.

My daughter, Meagan, got after me for complaining about my aging skin and sagging body. "Count your blessings, Mom. At least in this country, with our good health care, we have the option of growing old." That wasn't the response I was looking for. She was supposed to tell me I didn't look my age. Meagan's all I have left, but she's too busy for me. Young people don't realize there's no rewinding, no do-overs.

The speaker drones on, "Lilly loved life, her family and friends..."

I wonder what they'll say about me when I die. *Dot had a mediocre career in sales, a failed marriage, and a daughter who rarely communicated*...Lilly always knew how to cheer me up when I got down on myself, like I'm doing now.

| "As we look back on Lilly's life..." the speaker says.

When I look back on my life, memories merge into one another so it seems no time at all has passed. I recollect in flashes, bits and pieces, moments when time stood still.

One moment in utero, and the next, a tiny, squalling infant was laid on my bare chest. I placed my hand on my baby's soft skin, slick with amniotic fluid and blood, our combined blood. Meagan reached up and placed a warm, small hand on my face, like a greeting.

"Hush now, Darling," I said.

The baby quieted and looked at me with blue eyes. Her blurry first sight was me, her mother. Once together, now separate, we regarded each other. Meagan opened her mouth in the shape of an O, like she was going to ask me a question. Too soon they took her away, wrapped her in a blanket.

I thought I would have my baby with me forever. Now, I wait for occasional phone calls and infrequent visits. Until she has her own children, Meagan won't understand a mother's fierce love. In my grown daughter I recognize the infant who suckled from my breast, the six-year-old child who cuddled with me in bed, frightened by a nightmare. I see the heartbroken teenager, the young woman who I helped move to a university campus thousands of kilometres away, the person who will one day plan my funeral.

| The church service has started—standing, sitting, prayers, and Bible readings. I'm too distracted to pay attention. I haven't had a proper sleep since I heard the news. I'm trying to remember if I brushed my teeth this morning.

Everyone is standing up again, so I do, too. The priest is reading a passage from the Bible, but I'm not listening. Lilly was the religious one. I wonder what will happen to my soul when I'm done my time on Earth.

We all sit. The priest is talking now about Lilly, how she volunteered in the church in the St. Vincent de Paul ministry, helping the poor. I didn't know that about her. Now, I'll have to add that to the list of things that make Lilly a wonderful person...made, I mean. I wonder how I got to be sixty-three, but unlike Lilly, accomplished so little. My hands are shaking. I pick up the song book, just for something to hold onto.

Now the priest is talking about heaven. I clench my teeth. If he tells us, "Don't mourn her, she's now in a better place," I think I will scream and throw the song book at him. He doesn't though. He says, "If you miss Lilly, go ahead and cry. Tears are healing."

All around me, people are digging in pockets and purses for tissues, dabbing eyes and blowing noses. I stare into the distance, wishing I could feel something besides rage. I roll my neck to relieve the tension.

I'm hollow, like how I felt when I learned Meagan would be an only child. "You're just too old to have more children," the doctor told me, his face expressionless. I wanted to slap him for telling the truth. The doctor didn't know how deeply those words hurt me, even now, as I think back. Men can continue to father children into old age, as my ex did when he remarried, giving Meagan the little sister she always wanted.

The old regrets settle in while prayers are said for the repose of Lilly's soul. I wish I knew what went wrong with my marriage. Maybe if Paul and I had started our family sooner we'd still be together. The three unsuccessful attempts at in vitro fertilization, which resulted in miscarriages, took too much out of us physically, emotionally, financially. Meagan was our fourth attempt, our miracle child, born when I was forty-two. No matter how many times I tell myself that I should no longer mourn my unborn babies, I still long to hold them in my arms. I also long to hold Lilly. Like the babies I lost in miscarriage, I never got to say goodbye.

| We met in a first-year English literature class. I dropped out after second year. Lilly was brilliant in university, won awards as a pianist, became a chemical engineer, hiked the Grand Canyon in her fifties. She kept in shape, for all the good that did her.

Lilly was so sure about everything. She never dyed her hair or worried about wrinkles. Unlike me, she was able to accept her imperfections.

"You're beautiful on the inside," I told her.

"Are you calling me ugly?" she asked.

"No, I..." While I stammered and floundered, trying to apologize, she laughed. "Lighten up, Dot. Don't take yourself so seriously."

Now in my seventh decade, I still feel compelled to lie about my age, as if it's something to be ashamed of, like I've done something wrong by surviving multiple revolutions around the sun. Maybe it's time to accept my fate—my grey hair, crow's feet, arthritic knees, high cholesterol, high blood pressure, and the portly apple figure that puts me at risk for diabetes.

| My life used to revolve around my husband and child. I don't see my ex anymore, and Meagan has her own life, three provinces away. I can't be bothering her all the time. I need to adopt a lifestyle befitting my age but don't know what to do with myself anymore. I'd like to play golf or take night classes but can't afford the cost. Meagan told me to join a seniors' club, where I could mix with people my own age. I winced at the word "senior."

"That makes me sound old."

"Mom, you *are* old."

I think in her eyes I was always ancient. I was already forty-seven when Meagan started kindergarten.

"Is that your mother or your grandmother?" a classmate wanted to know.

I smiled at the innocence of children and avoided eye contact with the young moms in yoga pants and tank tops. They stood in a line, flaunting their taut butts and perky breasts, and hiding their smiles, watching me, waiting for the answer to the child's question.

"She's my mom," Meagan said.

I couldn't read the expression on my daughter's face, whether it was anger, confusion, or the sudden realization that her mother was different from the others. I wanted to disappear but held my head high as I left the classroom, pretending it didn't bother me. My face burned with humiliation for daring to be the age I was.

I never got used to it.

"It's nice of your grandma to take you out trick-or-treating."

"Is your mom working tonight? Is that why Grandma is bringing you to the Christmas concert?"

On the day of Meagan's high-school graduation and a week after my sixtieth birthday, my daughter came up behind me as I was putting on makeup in front of the mirror. She pressed her fresh young face against mine and put her arm around me. "Thanks for the dress, Mom."

I compared my greying hair to her beautiful tresses, the lines on my face beside her dewy skin, her hourglass figure beside my pumpkin-shaped torso. I forced a smile. "You're welcome."

I think I've been going through a mid-life crisis for the last twenty years.

| The Catholics are lining up to receive Communion, but I remain in my seat. I take a deep breath and focus my eyes on the closed coffin covered by a white sheet. *Lilly, you were my best friend. Why can't I cry? I'm going to miss you so much. I truly hope you are happy, wherever you are.*

Lilly was happy when she was alive, despite being widowed nine years ago and having a son with addiction issues. He and his sister sit next to me, looking forlorn.

Lilly once told me, "None of us are getting younger, Dot. We all have an expiration date. When your time comes, you gotta go. In the meantime, love the people around you, and for goodness sake, love yourself! Don't you know what an amazing person you are?"

"But I hate how unattractive I've become. We were both hot young things once upon a time, weren't we?" I ran my hand through my thinning hair. "I'm losing hair where I want it, growing hair where I don't want it." I took a sip of chardonnay.

She waved her hand at me. "So? Why do you care so much what other people think? Pluck your chin hair if it bothers you so much."

I laughed so hard I blew wine out of my nose.

| I smile at the memory. *I won't forget you, Lilly.*

The smoky-sweet smell of incense fills the church. Final prayers are being said.

People are getting up now to follow the casket out of the church.

Someone walks beside me. "It was a lovely service, wasn't it?" she asks.

"Oh, yes," I say. "It really made me think."

We all step outside to watch the pallbearers load the casket into the hearse. Lilly's son and daughter stand in front of me with arms linked. She rests her head on her brother's shoulder. The back doors of the hearse slam shut. I can no longer see the coffin. My chin begins to tremble. The car pulls away. They're taking Lilly to be cremated. My best friend's body will be burned in a furnace. I will never see her again.

I bring my hand to cover my mouth. Lilly's gone, forever.

I lose it. The tears I've held inside for four days come pouring out, along with wailing sobs. My shoulders are shaking, my throat aches, nose drips. Someone hands me tissues. I nod my thanks. Carly lets go of her brother and extends her arm to me. I run to them, wrapping my arms around Lilly's children. The three of us cling to each other and weep.

| I return to the parish hall for a cup of lukewarm coffee, an egg sandwich, and a cookie. I make promises to Lilly's children to stay in touch and then walk alone to my car. My heels tap, tap across the nearly empty parking lot. Sparrows twitter from the roof of the church. In a nearby playground children call to each other. I unlock my car, sit in front of the steering wheel and shut the door. Now, I hear only my inhales and exhales and the thuds of my heartbeats in my ears. *Is this how I will spend the rest of my days, with only myself for company?*

Next time I talk to Meagan I'll ask her for the name of that seniors' centre. I adjust my rear-view mirror to look at myself. My eyes are no longer red from crying, but I notice my grey roots are showing. It doesn't look that bad, really. I slap the steering wheel with the palm of my hand. "That's it!" I'm going to let my natural colour show.

Before backing out, I glance again in the mirror, running my fingers through my hair. I'm determined to follow Lilly's example, but that doesn't mean I can't try to look my best. I'll stop at the store when I'm feeling a little better, pick up hair dye and a pair of tweezers for my chin.

How I Got Old

DORA DUECK

I WAS FIFTY-EIGHT and my father eighty-seven when I made him laugh hard for the first time. He'd always been austere, a minister and teacher, not someone we children joked around with. Now he grinned at me and giggled. And giggled.

I'd been making a speech, basically "Use your walker!" because he kept trying to get around without it. He was in continual danger of falling, and Mom urged me to get his need to use the walker into his head.

But when I asked him what I'd just said, he replied, "I've forgotten already." This seemed hilarious to him.

My father had Alzheimer's and there was nothing to do except repeat and emphasize and laugh along. Mom looked on and smiled, but I could tell she was embarrassed. She struggled to understand and accept what was happening to her husband. I would have to coax her along, too, into their altered reality.

It felt strange to me, this bossy new role, me drilling him as if he were a child and he acting like one, me insisting to her it wasn't Dad but the disease that made him silly and forgetful. It set me above them both. Nevertheless, I was still their daughter. And, while my own aging was beginning to be obvious to me, relative to them I felt myself young.

My mother said, "You're so comical. Dad enjoyed that." Being praised by her in this maternal way made me feel younger as well.

Younger, yes, but besides their care I was busy with work and many other responsibilities, and the rush and busyness and duties of my days felt heavy. *I want my life to be about writing but seems it's about my parents,* I wrote in my journal. *I struggle to accept the interruptions, demands on my time, the weight of Dad's loss and Mom's burden.* Eventually we got my father into a personal care home. At the end of 2009, he died. This relieved the oversight I'd taken on in relation to him, but in the meanwhile, my mother grew increasingly reliant on my help, physically at first, on account of surgeries and subsequent immobility, then cognitively as she developed dementia. Since I was the only one of her eight children who lived nearby, much of the ongoing decision making and assistance, in her suite and later a seniors facility, devolved on me and my husband. It was a privilege to be close to her, and I loved her, but I can't deny I often chafed at the ongoing requests, from buying peanut butter to a bra to a bed, to coming over for visits, to sorting and disposing of things when she moved. I felt restless with it, like a teen longing to get out from under the thumb of the parental home.

This went on until 2015, she aging and me aging, but me far less aware of my aging than hers, for I still had many plans for the future—when the care of her might ease or be over, when I would finally have more time, when the pressure of life would soften! My husband planned to retire; I planned to complete writing projects I'd begun or dreamed of.

We also dreamed of moving closer to family. Our adult children had left our city and put down roots in Ontario and British Columbia.

Two of my sisters, residents of Saskatchewan, knew of our wish to be nearer family after retirement. They also knew I wouldn't leave Winnipeg as long as our mother was there and alive.

One day in the course of a visit, one sister asked, "Why don't we transfer Mom to a nursing home near us in Saskatchewan?"

I gasped. "Really? Is that even possible?" Such an option had never occurred to me.

She replied that it was; she'd checked.

"It's our turn," the other sister said.

I heard these words and something long-held in me released. *Oh my, oh my my my,* I breathed. The lift was palpable and for days I felt the joyous gift of it, a path coming true for me not because of Mom's death but because she and I could go on with life in other places.

We settled our mother into her new residence, and my husband and I decided to relocate to British Columbia. We put our house up for sale. We began to downsize our possessions. This took months, for we had two floors of house with three guest rooms and two offices, three bathrooms, bookshelves in three rooms with hundreds of books, as well as a detached workshop loaded with a lifetime of construction supplies and tools. Essentially, we Marie-Kondoed our entire existence, selecting what we needed for a retirement household and what sparked enough delight to keep. It was a great deal of work, and the memories attached to what we owned gripped us like a claw at times, but every item that left the property, from rakes to towels to extra tables and beds to our second vehicle, was another breath exhaled, another lightening.

At the end of our labours, the furniture and objects of our future life had been packed into an 8 × 8 × 10 container. We felt pleased with ourselves. Now we could drive away from a good past in one place and meet up with the container and our future in another, ready to unpack it into our apartment. I'd been freed of responsibility for both parents. We'd shed a house and a lot of stuff. We'd transferred property concerns to a landlord in exchange for a monthly cheque, and disentangled—by moving—from myriad connections and obligations and expectations. Our close friendships would be strong enough to continue via emails, phone, social media, and occasional visits.

Then I was startled by something I'd intuited but knew now with unexpected certainty, with force: I was old.

Old is as old does. Old cleans up. Old lets go.

Old is lightness.

Some of this was circumstantial, in the move up the generational ladder, neither parent physically present any more. Some was a surprise, in my sisters' generous gesture. Some was chosen, in facing and paring material accumulation. Those first months in BC, I would stand at the apartment balcony doors late evenings, staring over the parking lot below to the far street and wall of cedars beyond it, awed at where I'd arrived. When it rained, the streetlamps gleamed in the wet, and it all seemed magical to me, a vista of happiness.

I vowed to embrace my latest locations—both the geographical one and the life-stage one. I would claim the word old as modifier, older as preferred noun for what I am. I began a blog called *Chronicles of Aging* to observe and express who and where I was.

I found myself increasingly conscious of death, which statistically was the next big event of my life, and that prospect had a kind of lightness about it, too, a quality of lift and ease. I certainly wasn't pining for death, nor was it discernibly imminent, plus I still had all those plans, but the awareness of it, sooner rather than later, was an invitation to clear emotional garbage, to downsize at the psychic level. Ironically, while aging depleted my body energy, the inevitability of my end supplied energy for a vision of how to use my remaining time and resources. When I met older people who seemed resistant to the very idea of aging and death, I wanted to tell them that in my experience, acceptance was blessedly lighter than denial.

Soon after my husband and I moved to BC, we travelled to California where we volunteered for two weeks with Mennonite Disaster Service. We worked on a crew building a house for an uninsured couple who'd lost theirs in an area fire. We slept in bunks set up in a church hall, ate communally, showered in a trailer outside the building. One crisp morning I stepped out to walk to the showers. The air was cool, the stones under my feet rust red, and a thought popped into my head as if from outside, unattached to anything I'd been thinking. It was *you're almost done!*

Not done as in our volunteer assignment. Not some dissatisfaction with life. Just a glimpse of having done, imperfectly, and surely not yet finished, but done nevertheless, what I was born to do. I felt affirmed; glad. This too felt light, like the rise and wave of a kite in perfect wind.

Almost done. Old. Less now, but more than enough.

The moment was crystalline.

I could, of course, write a completely different story about aging than this one, and it would be true as well. I could write about it sneaking up on me, about the challenges I've experienced or can anticipate as an older. The wrinkles, the grey, the arthritic ache. Hearing loss, already under way. My fear of dependency, of dementia like my parents'. The small and not so small forgettings and less than stellar physical capacity. The subtle ageism, also in the writing world. Loneliness and envy. My husband's cancer and my sadness with—and for—him. We have our troubles, and I see that other people who are old have troubles, too. Yes, I could dump everything I've said so far on its head and say, persuasively, that life is as full and heavy as it was before I got old. Even heavier. I could say that aging is a load to carry.

But I can't convince myself. Not so far, at least, on account of how aging settled into its identity in me. I got lighter, discovered myself old, and the process felt backwards but exhilarating.

At sixty-nine, I like the time-place I'm in. And in spite of his health challenges, my husband says he likes it, too; he's amazingly reconciled to his life. For now, I have the companionship of a partner. He volunteers at a thrift store and Habitat for Humanity; I write. We share the housework. He's nourished by the sight of eagles; I find my Zen in reading or jigsaw puzzles. We walk. We feel at home in a local church. Our children are good people, independent and caring. We live simply but have enough money to do so. We have these advantages.

And there's a final argument in this for me. If old is as old does, which means letting go, what's been lightest all along is not included in the tally of what I've given up. Language—whether poetry or stories or memories in lists—tips us into the ineffable, as do art and music and nature and beauty and love. These have no weight but nevertheless fill and expand into every cavity where they're received. Laughter, too, is light and ineffable, and in spite of the grim diminishment my father's Alzheimer's forced on him and us, I think fondly now of how he laughed that day about my fake-stern scolding. He was old and he laughed, and I'd laughed along, as if reaching towards an odd but beguiling lightness he'd already achieved.

Adult Tween

PAULA E. KIRMAN

The joy of being ID'd

I went to a Bad Religion concert a few years ago. Although I was one of the older audience members, I felt at home among the youth adorned with faux hawks and facial piercings, many of whom hadn't been born when the legendary LA punk band first hit the scene in the '80s. Most of the guys in the band were older than fortyish me.

As I stood in line to enter the venue, I got ID'd. I think it was just the policy of the venue, but I still felt giddy. Why? Why should I feel happy about being taken for younger than my age?

I recall experiencing that same sense of joy and satisfaction many years earlier when I was mistaken for being older. When people thought I was already in university, although I was still in high school. And then when people thought I was in grad school, although I was still an undergrad.

Getting older was something to be desired. It meant growing up, finishing school. It meant getting a chance to see the world, to experience love, to do whatever fun things real adults got to do.

Then, somewhere along the line, I began internalizing the message that getting older was A BAD THING. I would be judged by society not on my talents and abilities but my age. It could be a reason to be rejected for jobs, partners, opportunities. Those who identified as men would not be subject to harsh criticisms for their wrinkles, grey hair, or advancing years. Society viewed them as experienced, desirable. We who identify as women were seen by society as used up, worn out, done.

It didn't seem fair. How could anyone be judged poorly based on something as natural as growing older? I made my decision. I was going to rock it—keep on working in the arts, perform music, write, and not let it faze me that every year my colleagues seemed to be getting younger.

Ma'am

"Can I help you, Ma'am?"

That dreaded word that almost everyone who presents as a woman hears at some point.

I don't exactly recall the circumstances of my first "ma'am," but I know it happened long before the silver streaks in my hair become as prominent as they are now.

I learned from an early age not to take ma'am with offense. It's how some people were taught to refer to women in a respectful manner.

But not just any women. Older women. Women who have matured to the point where they are owed respect befitting their perceived age. Did I just use the word "matured?" That's almost always used as a euphemism for "old."

"Don't call me ma'am," I have heard some of my friends say. Although I have not gone quite as far as verbally objecting— yet—I have considered it. At the very least, I understand where my friends are coming from. The word not only implies an assumption about my age, but it is a binary term that makes an assumption about a person's gender. I'm of the mindset that we don't need to add a gender qualifier to say "excuse me" or ask if a person would like to sit down.

Interestingly, I have witnessed an objection from a man to being called "sir" only once. And for the same reason as many women have given. He didn't want to be labelled or identified as an old man, because being old is A BAD THING. Or, at least that's how he saw it.

Caught in the middle

I'm in my mid-forties. Although in many ways I still feel the tugs of youthful energy, it's been a long time since I could be classified as young, in the traditional sense. However, I'm still a ways away from old age and all of those things that come with it: Retirement. Federal pension. The seniors' discount.

But wait—I have already experienced the latter. Not that long ago, I was examining a receipt from a store and noticed I had been given the seniors' discount. I had already left the store and had no way to inquire why this benefit had been bestowed upon me. Another assumption.

On the other hand, I've gotten comments about my looks being on the other end of the spectrum. "You look so much younger than in this picture," said the bank teller after I showed her my driver's license. (And really—does anyone look good in one of those photos?)

I guess that's why my stage of life is called middle age. In comparative terms, I'm the adult equivalent of a tween. In realistic terms, how my age is interpreted depends on the others in my immediate social circle—and the eyes of my beholders. When I attend concerts or social actions and the majority of the other people there are in or barely out of their twenties, I'm the elder stateswoman. However, when I got involved in community organizing and advocacy, I started to attend planning meetings with people ten to twenty years older than me. I was the kid in the group, despite being well into my thirties. As we have all aged since then, I'm still the kid, as absurd as that seems now. I am caught between two worlds.

The vanishing middle-aged woman

I suppose in some ways I should be glad to be called ma'am or noticed as the young one at meetings. At least I am being noticed. Several of my peers have commented that women tend to vanish when we hit middle age. We're not seen or heard unless we make a concentrated effort to raise our voices. Why is this? Maybe it is because younger people are seen as outshining us professionally and socially. Maybe it is because many of us are caught in the sandwich between taking care of our young families and taking care of our elders, leaving time for little else. Or maybe society simply values youthful energy over wisdom and experience.

40: The dividing line

More words I could use to describe my present state would be "change" and "denial."

I've known about my greying hair for a while. My first grey hair was actually in my eyebrow. I was twenty-four. I plucked it out and screamed. I calmed down, showed it to my mother, and became offended that she did not want to keep it with my archive of firsts—first haircut, first lost teeth, and so on.

"It's not the same," she said. I didn't understand why. To me, this was something significant, something representing a stage of life.

At the same time, it was freaking me out. In fact, twenty-five was my hardest birthday. There was something about the whole quarter-of-a-century reality that seemed quite intimidating. I recall a time when eighteen, the legal age of adulthood in Alberta, seemed a long way off. Twenty-five seemed out of reach. Forget about thirty, the age at which, I'd always been told, women started to lose their appeal and sexual power. Then forty—forty was OLD.

In fact, forty seems to be society's benchmark between young and old. A popular magazine in Edmonton and Calgary has an annual Top 40 Under 40 award, as if to imply that achievements made at a younger age somehow merit extra significance. Most young-adult groups in churches and other organizations begin in the twenties and have forty as the upper cut-off. The last day that you're thirty-nine, you're still part of the group. On your birthday, that's it—you're an outcast.

I find such age groupings odd—someone in their twenties can be in a very different stage of life than someone in their late thirties. I wouldn't want to be in my twenties again. It was a time of much emotional upheaval and unpacking of past trauma. Although for a while I dreaded turning thirty, that decade was memorable for finding myself in spiritual and creative ways. My forties, so far, have been a time of continued growth and coming into my own as an individual.

A lightning bolt of grey

When I turned forty, I threw a birthday party for myself at my favourite bar and almost missed it due to coming down with a horrendous bout of the flu the week before. The flu. In July. I was too weak to shower for a few days, which of course were extremely hot, and in the middle of everything I got my period. I lay there in bed sweaty and delirious, looking at my walls, my books, and my stuffed animals, while thinking, "Is this it?" I thought something monumental was supposed to happen when a person turned forty, and all I had was fever and a skin rash.

And really, nothing much changed in terms of my life of writing, community organizing, and maintaining some semblance of a personal life. But the grey hairs kept coming, and I tried to ignore them for as long as possible. Until one day I couldn't. "I need to show you something," I said to my friend in a panicked tone.

"What's wrong?" she asked.

I showed her a photo on my phone, a picture that someone had snapped of me and posted on social media. I was at an event filming, my profile to the other person's camera, and behind my ear was a ribbon of white, looking like a lightning bolt. "This," I said, pointing to my grey hairs in the photo. "Do I really have that?"

My friend, who is a few years older than me, burst out laughing. That evening, she sent me a copy of the photo, using her creativity to create a streak of purple in the area in question. I was amused, while at the same time I contemplated colouring my hair for real.

Then I thought about it. A lot. I decided that whatever grey hairs I have, I earned—and I've since learned to accept them. Why should I cover over my natural state to try to fulfill someone else's standard of beauty? I've struggled with this all my life. I have never worn much makeup and started to grab hand-me-downs from my older brother long before gender-neutral clothing was a thing. I've also struggled with the double standard in our society when it comes to physical appearance and body shaming towards men—it happens, but not as often, and not with as much vitriol. Just look at age-gap relationships—rarely does romance between older men and much younger women make anyone bat an eye. While older women with younger men is becoming more socially acceptable than in the past, it still isn't regarded as the norm.

Why can't we automatically view changes like greying hair and wrinkles as natural?

Living and loss

But aging is more than physical and cosmetic changes. Aging brings with it the recognition that growing older brings growing loss. We are survivors as we watch friends, family members, and partners pass from this world.

Recently, I lost my mother. The grief is still in its acute stage, with alternating bouts of shock, disbelief, and sadness. For my mother, old age meant an ever-increasing number of health issues.

Losing a parent is something most of us have to deal with at some point. It's one of those universal experiences that connect us as humans. So for me, aging now also means a future of navigating unfamiliar territory without the most influential woman in my life. It also makes me keenly aware of my own mortality.

Ironically, even in the advanced stages of ill health, my mother would be told that she looked good for her age. She did. However, while I know she felt complimented by those remarks, I am sure she would much rather have felt good for her age.

It's a fallacy that looking good necessarily translates into being healthy, although that is society's message. Youth, attractiveness, and health are all inextricably intertwined—and it simply isn't true for everyone. Looking good for your age is completely subjective. In the end, how we look as we get older comes down to little more than genetics and certain life choices. Even then, sometimes it's just plain luck. And maybe, in the end, there are more important things to pay attention to than how I or others look.

So here I sit, between the two extremes of the memories of youth and the anticipation of the years to come. My goal is to stay focused and stop looking at the outward signs of aging, but rather look to the inward signs of individuality, and what it means to be someone who identifies as a woman in a changing world.

Shuffle

JANE CAWTHORNE

70. If, somehow, I live this long, I imagine my posture is
good. I'm steady on my feet. This is what I want for myself
more than anything. I will credit all the yoga. But don't
ask me to touch my toes. I have never been flexible. A few
internal organs are missing, the ones I can easily do without.
The scars stay covered, except for two. The surgical scar on
my neck is white and deep and kept me wearing scarves for
a while. I don't care anymore. The jagged line over my right
eye, faded to near invisibility by the time I was fifty, makes
my lid droop now. I am no judge of my own face, but my
hands are those of a seventy-year-old. My so-called white skin
is spotted with evidence of my lifetime of carelessness in the
sun. I tell people I'm eighty.

15. I am not the kind of girl who is told she is pretty. If
someone has told me so, I haven't heard it. I am a smart girl.
That is enough. That is better. "Looks fade," says my mother.

38. My employment puts me in the public eye. I go to an
expensive salon to learn what I have never known how to do:
fix my hair and put on makeup. I buy thick, black-rimmed

glasses so that I am distracted by them when I see my own face in the news. I can tolerate the exposure. Barely. I learn never to wear white on TV.

5. I sit on the edge of the bathtub and watch my mother put her face on. I learn what to worry about—dark circles under the eyes, red in the wrong places, eyelashes that are too short, lips that are too pale. She is never satisfied.

33. In the photograph, I am twenty-eight years old, tanned, and smiling on the deck of a sailboat. I'm wearing a neon-pink, one-piece bathing suit with high-cut legs and a low-cut back. When I first saw the photograph, I silently chastised myself for thinking I could get away with that suit. Legs like tree trunks, I thought. But now, five years too late, I appreciate myself. There is a lesson to be learned.

50. Some lessons are easily forgotten. When someone tries to take my picture, I wave my hands in front of my face and joke that I am in the witness-protection program. I stole that joke from my mother.

42. I am still alive. I am bald, skeletal and weak. I don a hat and shuffle to the grocery store. An acquaintance sees me standing over the bananas and says, "Where have you been? I haven't seen you for ages." She looks me up and down and can only see how thin I am. "You look amazing," she says. Thin is good, even when it means you might die.

30. I have traded a tight body for a lumpy body and a baby. It's a good deal.

8. My older sister is the pretty one. This is widely acknowledged.

48. Someone asks me how old I am. I say, "Fifty-six," and get a compliment. From then on, when someone asks my age, I tell the story about how I added almost a decade to my age and earned a compliment and then I give them a number. No one knows if I am still lying. I like the ambiguity.

56. Strangers stop me on the street to ask me questions all the time. I take this as evidence that I look friendly. This pleases me.

She shops at the Sally Ann and Value Village

JOAN CRATE

not so much because of the bargain prices
as stretched waistbands and faded prints,
the soothing scent of stale detergent
cheek to cheek with old sweat.

Worn fabric whispers release to her skin
and she knows she can never go back
to stiff zippers and starchy collars,
loud colours screaming *here I am!*

These days she can barely endure
a brief brush let alone a scouring,
opts for baby shampoo and soft bristles
before bedtime flannel and down-filled

slumber. Some of us—made-over
and multi-tasking, throbbing feet
in stylish shoes—wonder if she knows something
we don't—how the spirit weathers, blisters

and weeps under tension, expectation
and tight deadlines. We grow heavy
as over-ripe fruit,
                    can lose our grip—
                    fall

ENOUGH!

Part of the Furniture

ARITHA VAN HERK

THE TALKATIVE AUSTRALIAN WOMAN on the plane
from Paris to Montpellier wants me to solve her "cerebral
enhancement" puzzle, an app on her phone that involves
making words out of scrambled letters. "You're a professor,"
she says. "It'll be easy for you."

How she has maneuvered this information out of me is
baffling, although her persistence persists. I occasionally
play Scrabble on my own device, but I am on the whole unin-
terested in puzzles and the "brain games" that will improve
mental health and stave off incipient softening of my faculties. I'd rather read or gamble or cook or lift weights.

When I can't decode the poser she shoves in my direction,
she says, "How old are you? You look like you're my age. I'm
sixty-three."

"Some Canadians," I tell her, "are reticent about discussing
age, income, and cultural background."

But she won't let up. "Are you sixty? Are you fifty-five? Are
you older?"

She is on her way to Montpellier to join a group of friends
who will be bouncing around France, from there to Paris,
then Nice and Grenoble, to follow the games of FIFA, the

Women's World Cup. "We're their cheering section, the Matildas," she announces, but there is nothing waltz-like about her, and her knuckles are as bruised as a bouncer's. "We've been champions three times. I'm sixty-three."

"Are you a soccer player then?" I ask.

"Oh no," she says. "Golf's my game."

She wants beer, and the flight attendant hands her a Kronenbourg. She complains that it is too warm but downs it efficiently, and when the cart passes again, demands another.

"No more," says the crisply scarfed Air France warden, as if beer were dangerous.

"Wouldn't you like French wine instead?" I ask.

"Beer," she says. "I like cold cold beer." And she belches. But her word game fortunately distracts her, and even while she mutters over its frustrations, she is ready to jump out of her seat when we touch down. "No matter how old you are," she declares, "you look pretty good for your age."

For all her prying, her guileless energy heartens me. She travels alone, she follows women's football, she is unafraid of speaking bad French overlain with an Australian accent, and I imagine she will find infinite varieties of beer, will test them all the way through France. I am sure she will be the rowdiest and loudest of the Matildas in the stands, definitely a RAGER—a person who parties long and hard, in Australian argot—and no granny at all.

But her bald curiosity about my age compounds the many conjectures I now confront, the heft assigned to numbers, the measurement of accumulated years, the tired cliché of "rumpled older ladies." And it harkens to the antipathetic clinical language attached to women: perimenopause, hot flashes, useless ovaries, transition, serotonin, displeasure, fertility, pathological rage, sexual irrelevance, disorientation. Which generalized blueprint, *prima facie*, is not always applicable. I experience no hot flashes, no pathological rage, and no disorientation.

And if the age factor buttresses the ill-considered assumption that we are not "of use," I am well aware of my use-value—I am asked for hundreds of favours, letters, recommendations, donations, assistance, and supports every year. Perhaps not "of use," but of value.

Women of my generation have much to say about being invisible and despised, about the expectation that we will be reticent and stoic, that we should "grow old gracefully," which translates as silent, compliant, and inconspicuous.

Certainly, contempt seems inescapable. The slight sneer and lift of the shoulder from my younger colleagues with a comment about retiring—"And when do you intend to retire?" Which opens the unfinished half of their sentence, "and get out of the way?" The ungracious comment of a supposed friend, a man, who seeing me at an event after six months of completing three projects, battling a bad flu, and being flat-out exhausted, informed me, "You look old." The scorn of a woman in my bootcamp class, dismissing my space, as if wondering why I am there at all—although I can kick her ass in weightlifting. Her dismissal mitigated by the instructor saying to me, very quietly and directly, without evasion, "You can do it. You are a strong woman." I treasure that instructor's confidence, his laughter and joy in the work the body can do—all bodies, all capabilities and shapes and ages. My body is not fragile, and I am not ashamed of my sturdiness.

So, what, I ask, looking around my busy, high-test world, are my "signs of age"? Are they a physical designation or a facial erasure, the lines that I have accumulated, the countenance that shows I live happily and well? I cannot help but think of the television show, *Lie to Me*, where Tim Roth

rzes micro-expressions to read people's faces for infor-
on, pain, concealment, or lying. It would be fascinating
to apply this analysis to older people, to decipher scorn or
delight, pleasure or pain or surprise, in flashes of emotional
leakage, how every experience has carved an intricate etching
on "the faces that we wear to meet the faces that we meet."
Ah, Prufrock. Now, he was afraid of age. And he had to dare
himself merely to bite into a peach.

The physicality of age is fascinating. Our bodies change,
our ears and our noses grow. Why? Gravity, perhaps, a
weighty force. The research on cortisol, "perceived age," and
facial appearance, not to mention the body's outward aspect,
is apparently predicated on stress markers. Those of us who
face or who embrace challenges, which leads to increased
cortisol output, are likely to experience higher levels of stress
than those who practice "water off a duck's back" responses,
which subsequently has an effect on appearance—we are
more likely to grow "haggard."

Those who have worked long and hard are expected to
resemble the paintings of old women, "The Fisherman's
Mother" (by Helen Mabel Trevor) or "Whistler's Mother,"
gnarled and sagging and infinitely patient, and only too often
depicted dozing over a book. This attribution of patience
arouses in me a fierce impatience. No one is more impatient
than a woman aware that time is fleeting, and who resents
every wasted moment. I confess, that is the one aspect of
growing older that I suffer from most: severe and undiluted
impatience. And in its midst, the dual recognition that
contentment is both less and more desirable than expected.

| I face now certain facts. The distance of the world from
those who grow old is a measure of incipient apprehension.
When we see traces of aging, we resist, hesitate, insistently

revert to a desire to be nineteen forever as a denial of inevitable seasoning. I return again and again to Julian Barnes's metatextual biography, *Nothing to be Frightened Of*, a meditation on death, language, and the process of aging. A fascinating and erudite book, it roams from his family to writers and composers, as well as his own creative explorations. He declares that he has two rules for his writing life: "no dreams and no weather." He puts the rules down to his irritation with "significance," that we attribute to dreams and weather more metaphorical weight than is warranted when we read fiction or life-writing.

I concur with the heavy-handed obviousness of dreams certainly, but the weather? There I believe Barnes is wrong, because weather measures age and time, and as we grow older, we check the visage of the sky more and more. It looks good outside, we say. I should forgive Barnes; he doesn't live in Alberta, where it snows in June at least every other year. He resides in London, where the weather is a persistent, grey overcast.

But I am, with Barnes, fascinated by how we occupy the body, how it becomes over time less tangible than imaginary. Does growing older increase indifference or induce a weird serenity, acceptance of the hazards of living, embracing the conjunction of accident and mystery, the desire to be hit by a speeding truck, the temptation of jumping off a bridge.

Once she has gulped that warm beer, finished her word game, and before we touch down, the Australian interrogator confounds me with her next question. "Have you ever had a near-death experience?"

"No." I say this hesitantly. What the hell's next?

"What do you think happens to us after we die?"

I shrug. "Dust. Compost."

"Oh surely," she says, "you don't believe that there's nothing. Don't you think a trace of our pneuma continues?"

I'm surprised again by her using such a complex philosophical word. "We don't know," I say cautiously.

"I know," she states as determinedly as she asked for another beer. "I believe there's another side. I want to have an out-of-body encounter. I really want a near-death experience."

"Aren't we having one now?" I suggest dryly. "Flying through the air."

"See?" she says. "You believe in a spiritual dimension."

"No, I don't."

"Not even that some spark continues, that our life force steps out into the universe?"

"No." I say this more firmly, grateful that the seatbelt light has come on and we are descending. "I want to live now, in the moment, not hope for some Nirvana later."

I don't tell her that I used to live on a cul de sac named Nirvana, so called by a somewhat romantic city developer. I am sure she would interpret that as a sign.

And after all, who wants immortality? It would be overwhelming to imagine living longer than one's body wishes to live. There is the crux, the body and its crumbling infrastructure, its desire to close in on its own memory and function. A narrowing of the focal distance, how we look and what we see.

The pervasive complaint, once women cross fifty, is of not being seen, becoming invisible. This is most evident in the contemporary habit of people walking without lifting their heads from their devices, so that the world has become much more of an obstacle course. Those so engrossed leave the dodging and weaving to those of us who do watch where we are going. I have a method for dealing with this rudeness.

I simply keep walking and do not step out the way. Why is it up to me to perform the avoidance dance, to prevent the collision? I do not. And because I am strong, and prepared, inevitably the other person gets the brunt of the bump. And I get an apology, cursory or not.

As for invisibility, I rather cherish this power, have always yearned to disappear, have written about disappearance in many of my books and stories, have disappeared my characters and disappeared myself. In disappearing, I can become more than I am. By avoiding regard, I am less present but more powerful. Invisibility argues the temptation of erasure, the sleight of hand that puts me in the magician's shoes. I am no longer assistant to the illusionist, I am the one conjuring myself into a space where I have complete freedom to be invisible, joyfully invisible, free to say and do what I wish, without recrimination or its pedagogy. Most of all, I am interested in turning my experience into art, words, an engravement and capture of my pain and pleasure, whereas younger writers obscure those aspects, or try to decorate them. We may outlive what we lose, but the losses of experience have less to do with diminishment than with increased liberty.

There are frustrations, elements that direct my impatience. I have lived long enough to have encountered in my lifetime thousands of people, family, friends, acquaintances, students, colleagues, fellow artists, truly thousands. I recognize people's faces, and even their gestures, but I fail to remember their names, although this has little to do with senescence—I have never remembered names readily. The expectation that I will is impatience-provoking. I have known in my life hundreds of Jeffs and Annes and Johns and Isabelles and Ians and Jordans, and only if I am reminded of first and last names and context can I connect that person with my experience of them, although they certainly seem to remember me. So much for invisibility. I have taken to asking deliberately, "How do I know you?" and demanding more information, first and last names, the dinner party, the year, the workshop, the setting. One aspect of growing older is the wish for everyone to wear a name tag.

But the greatest irritation of my advancing experience is the increasing diminishment of nuance and precision—not mine but others'. My intolerance for sloppy language, poor grammar, and lack of professionalism increases every day. I yearn for nuance, complexity combined with subtlety, experience with freshness, the language of intelligent discernment and thought. I have become a "grammar police-woman," wanting to discipline blurred outbursts of partial sentences interrupted by "you know," "like," and "thing," filler language, valley babble, discourse markers, hedges, substitution words, and overall ineloquence. I crave complete sentences, unusual vocabulary, and the quality of thought of an Oxford lecturer. And I am bound to be disappointed, a life and language disappointment that will doubtless never be rectified. Although rage I will.

Other and smaller vexations trip me. The discovery that as one grows older, a woman's struggle is less against strong men than against weak men. I encountered on another airplane trip a man who explained mansplaining to me—now that was a *mise en abyme*, exceptionally annoying but after the fact hilarious.

And so, I watch, explore, rummage, delve. Actively. What matters? Should I be afraid of loneliness? I have never minded being alone, believing Marianne Moore's line that "the cure for loneliness is solitude." Ageism? It will certainly take on a different dimension as postprandial "baby boomers" grow in numbers and refuse to be coagulated, the sheer volume of that generation redirecting the realms of expectation, the market, the demands of accessibility, the adjustment of noise levels, and the ease of speed.

And maybe my Australian seat-mate is right. Nothing is ever over. There is time to lobby—for good pockets in women's clothing, for a personal laugh track, for the elegance of flat shoes, for brilliant revenge, for passionate execution.

"There is time to murder and create." Yes, indeed, Prufrock.

I am less patient than I was at fifty.

I am stronger than I was at forty.

I am smarter than I was at thirty.

I am wiser than I was at twenty.

I am more furious than ever.

I refuse to be "a senior." I am senior, period.

I have earned that right.

Je fais partie des meubles. And while I am part of the furniture, I am neither immobile nor retro.

Kissing Kismet Goodbye

MONI BRAR

I've failed
so utterly
so completely
they say,
tsk tsk-ing lips clicking
smug eyes batting false eyelashes.

they feed me mouthfuls of pity
like bite-sized samosas
spiced with cumin
and sympathy.
they dance around me
Bollywood style
bedazzled by their own splendour
showcasing midriffs
with scars to prove
their ability to create.

I'm so tired
carrying men and mothers and this
always uphill
no time for rest
rest is for the weak
or is it the wicked?
I am both.

an old crone,
barren
with crow's feet
where birds used to alight
and dance on my face
in the corners of my eyes,
before Miss was replaced with Ma'am.
Damn.
Grand Dame.
Grand ma, I will never be.

Lookin' Back

LORRI NEILSEN GLENN

FOR THE LOVE OF GOD, for the love of that pure young woman—did you look at her? The one with blonde hair to her ass, a twenty-two-inch waist, the one who never needed a lick of lipstick, who wore any old thing because everything fit and nothing is as attractive as smooth skin, bright eyes, a lithe body, and the energy of a gazelle. Didn't she burn with promise? Heads turned as she approached, eyes lingered, but she kept her head down, having learned the hard way the perils of looking back.

Decades on, she notices she is rarely noticed, she could be a hedge or a lamppost, no one looks back to see if she is looking back to see, she is no longer the muse for a poet, the fertile prize, the spirited gal in the lyrics of a Buck Owens song.

"Men look at women. Women watch themselves being looked at." A man wrote that. John Berger tells us we turn ourselves into objects, into surveyed beings who move, dress, gesture, paint ourselves for the male gaze, looking at ourselves as they might look at us. We subject ourselves to being objects. Ah! A man who understands the trap, understands the burden the world places on women.

(A man who speaks for us.)

(Of course, he does. Objects can't figure out things for themselves.)

But here it comes. And it comes in waves. The day she realizes she can pry off the clammy fingers of scrutiny, the day she strides past the whistle-free construction site, her old bone house intact, hers alone. She is dressed for comfort in an easy style she's learned to love, her hair trim, a touch of makeup on her eyes, but never because

she hopes he—

she hopes they—

does this make my rear end—?

If the mirror pleases today, no one else matters. And you? Yes, you whose eyes gloss over her presence in the grocery aisle. She knows you pay her no mind, she blends into the bread shelf, the stack of canned peas, but in turn, she's free from the lingering hand, sly leer, the eyes' swift assessment head to toe, checking for cleavage.

And almost free from the unwanted and awkward breast-smashing hug. Almost.

She strides past the coffee aisle, a fugitive from the land of fuckability, knowing even if you looked past the broad hips or the gauzy wrinkles, even if you were the rare soul who desired a lived-in body and wise eyes, it's too late. She'll be polite, of course, but time is short, and before you can take a second look, she's off somewhere doing things it took her years to realize she wanted to do.

She has picked up a brush, or walks in the forest alone, or sits at a busy intersection with charcoal and blank pages. She's writing a book, arranging flowers, knitting for babies in the NICU. She's reading philosophy, organizing an environmental movement. She's living with another woman. She's travelling the Canadian North or writing disability policy or volunteering for medical research.

Listen. Can you hear that deep sigh of contentment when she settles in to do the thing? Can you see the corners of her mouth lift lightly?

Listen. You're lookin' back to see, but she's not. It's plain to see she's focused on a new horizon: dwindling days. Jewels of time that glow brighter now. She has realized a harvest she hadn't known she'd planted. Walk on by; nothing to see here. Only a woman looking forward.

Gathering. Taking stock, making lists. Naming names. Finally, yes, finally. Not only does she have a room of her own, she has become her own room.

Now she can get some goddamned work done.

Well Preserved

E. D. MORIN

FROM MY CAFÉ TABLE, I watch them enter. I observe them huddle together and stand in line, habituated as I am from hours of watching screens, those miniature crystal-line savannas, everything a game preserve now. The distinct sounds of Korean, *seyo* and *nida*, the musical lilt of their tongues flow between them. One woman's hair is blonde dyed with brushstrokes of green. The palest of greens. Grey green. I admire the strange boldness of it. I wonder at her matching sweater, the mint green Melton-cloth coat. I could never wear those hues and be beautiful, not even when I was young. It reminds me of Anne Shirley and her green hair.

And I recall my friend from Incheon and her affection for the young orphan Anne who was sent to live at Green Gables. My friend said she'd read that book countless times growing up, the Korean translation first. Later, the original. The redheaded heroine's hair-dyeing debacle was especially funny, she said. Funny and sadly moving.

Observing these young women from where I sit, I grudg-ingly concede that they would be beautiful no matter what they wore, no matter how they messed with their hair. Even feisty Anne with an e and her botched dye job would have been beautiful; I see that now. But why aren't women of a certain age valued in the same way? Why isn't natural grey becoming? When a petal turns, its vibrant colour fades, its seeds scatter. And that's it, I suppose. Instead of coming into themselves, women of a certain age camouflage their nature. Hide their wisdom.

I ponder this, and I realize that the age of scattering is not so certain.

A few years ago, when I stopped dyeing my hair and got a pixie cut, like the one I had when I was seven, suddenly the white became prominent. It created a ring of light around my face. I never expected that this would be occasion for commentary, but even the barista at my favourite coffee shop managed to gush about how well preserved I was. Her sincerity made me realize she intended this as a compliment. For a while, I even thought I might embrace her words. Start a canning business. Labels for jams and jellies that included a photo of myself. The brand name Well Preserved. But I've yet to follow through on this.

And now that I've let my hair tend to white, I can't help but notice that women eye me sharply. Not all of them, but some. As if I've broken the natural order. And then one day a defender approaches me. She says, your hair is subversive. Initially, I'm flustered and all I can do is thank her, but later I wonder. Why is natural hair subversive? Dyeing is a such waste of time. The procedure always made my neck sore. It honestly never looked right on me, and besides, all that swirling dye entering the watershed? It made me feel guilty.

Today, I notice a new anti-aging business in my neighbourhood. The sandwich board announces, *Tired of looking tired? Try Botox!* There's that ludicrous word anti-aging. There's the scolding tone. Either I'm letting my jowls sag, exposing my wrinkles, revealing my capacity to decline, or I am NOT.

I stop and glare at the board. I bristle. *Tired?* Tired suggests worn out or kaput. It suggests no longer valued, like baggy trousers when everyone else is wearing tights. It suggests I've been fooling myself by letting my wrinkles get out of hand, and never mind my white bangs. The internal dialogue continues. But I'm not tired. Wrinkles are my hard-won trophies. This is just me, entirely me. I'm just being myself. At this point, I somehow resist the urge to go inside and inform the staff that there's no antidote to aging, that their sham version of it is alien and unmoving, that no matter what they do to try to prevent it, we are ALL getting older by the minute.

Take Earth. Our home is a little worse for wear of late. Places that are too dry. Places that are too wet. Systems declining. It reminds me of myself, only on a near-unfathomable scale. Lifespan, for instance. Scientists say that our home is four and half billion years old. They say that Earth has reached middle age and will soon (in a few million years?) begin her decline. Eventually, by age twelve billion, she will be no more. Absorbed by the sun. How to get my head around such vast timespans? Who can relate to a billion?

I can't. All I know is that the last few hundred years (a comparative blip, apparently) have been particularly hard on the poor dame. On her glaciers, her corals. Her fish and fowl. But who's to say how she's really holding up? Earth has survived meteor collisions, after all. Pole reversals. Earthquakes and ice ages and continental drifts. She's having a tough time now because of our shenanigans, but our human gig may soon be up. So maybe, like after a huge bender, she'll simply take a rest after we're gone and then bounce right back. Flourishing like her old self. Looking good again for her age.

And then there's Anne. I wonder why she hated her red hair. Shame, likely. Shame that followed her to Avonlea, so that when her schoolroom antagonist called her Carrots, she struck him over the head with her slate (a primitive precursor to our screens). But even with all her fiery resistance, she still tried to banish the red, still coveted raven locks.

What did we learn from Anne Shirley, really?

One More Word

JOYCE HARRIES

if I hear one more word
about once you hit seventy
it's all downhill
as though at midnight of that birthday
a switch clicks
and each body system turns to one another and says
you first   I'll take my turn
and one at a time
hip joints seize
knees creak
arteries clog
earlobes lengthen
hair thins
nose drips
face lines deepen
eyebrow hairs turn wiry
gastric juices erupt
teeth crack
corneas wobble
pupils wrinkle
eyes dim
names elude memory

if I hear one more advising word
about the pills
try gingko biloba
vitamin E, lutein, glucosamine and probiotics
what about coenzyme Q10, bilberry
think about going vegan
don't drink coffee after noon
or go in the sun to pick nasturtiums unless you wear sunblock
and who do you think you are
painting your living room chartreuse when everyone else's
    is off-white
did you start wearing red when your husband died

if I hear one more teasing word
about grandchildren's pictures
floating in piles in purses
at lunch they're passed 'round like birthday cards
and the young waitress rolls her eyes, when we divide the bill
hoping our tip will be generous enough
we've had our decaf skim lattes
our salads and   no desserts thanks

and if I hear one more word
about how bad it is to age
I will throttle that person
probably a man
who can't flow with life's patterns
needs to stay young
marry dot com executive
has new family
silly old goat
why didn't he do it
right the first time

if I hear one more envious word
about that contemporary of ours
you know
the one who runs with a pack of runners
the one who climbs mountains
boyfriends in three cities
skin taut
teeth white
hit a hole in one
can drink most men under the table

if I hear one more word about some other women who
    are aberrations
who don't age
do they secretly spend one day a week in bed
like titled English authors once did
and bathe in chamomile or sea salt
have private masseuses
silk undergarments between lavender sachets
bed sheets slippery satin
bedrooms overlooking parks
morning tea tray holding yellow roses

if I hear one more aging comment
I will reply reasonably
      prolonging my prime of life

yes
some of what you say is true

but oh

        to wake   stretch   hear birdsong
        creak out of bed
        look in the mirror

yes, I'm still here

        bring in the paper
        put on the kettle
        whole wheat bread in toaster
        slather marmalade

embrace the day

Notes

"The Fixable" by Sharon Butala
The definition of legal blindness is from Alberta Health. Statistics on the ages of people with full or partial blindness are from a 2013 World Health Organization Report.

"Sundowning" by Debbie Bateman
Naomi Feil developed the Validation Method as a way to treat patients with dementia and help their families. The method is outlined in *The Validation Breakthrough: Simple Techniques for Communicating with People with Alzheimer's and Other Dementias*, third edition, by Feil and Vicki de Klerk-Rubin (Health Professions Press, 2012).

"Body Composition" by Wendy McGrath
A Class in Greek Poise is one of the many one-woman dramas Ruth Draper wrote and performed internationally throughout her adult life. It appears on pages 175–180 in *The Art of Ruth Draper: Her Dramas and Characters* (Oxford University Press, 1980).

"Rarification" by Vivian Hansen
Vivian Hansen's essay "Coming of Age" appears on pages 97–98 of *Deeply into the Bone: Re-inventing Rites of Passage*, edited by Ronald L. Grimes (University of California Press, 2000). Grimes's comment on "Coming of Age" appears in the same book.

"The Shave" by Rona Altrows

This story won the *Alberta Views* magazine short-story contest and first appeared in the December 2019 issue of *Alberta Views*. It was also shortlisted for an Alberta Magazine Publishers' Award. It can be found at https://albertaviews.ca/the-shave/.

"Telescoping" by Julie Sedivy

This piece won the Jon Whyte Memorial Essay Award. The writer cites the following works: *Where I Live Now: A Journey Through Loss and Love to Healing and Hope,* by Sharon Butala (Simon & Schuster Canada, 2017); and "Taking Time Seriously: A Theory of Socioemotional Selectivity," found on pages 165–81 of *American Psychologist,* 54, no. 3 (1999).

"Well Preserved" by E. D. Morin

The writer adapted parts of this essay from the following previous publications: "Hey Menopause, Tap Refresh!" which appears in *New Forum* (Loft on EIGHTH, 2019); and "Well Preserved," in the Short Story Dispenser (Calgary Public Library, Short Edition, 2019), and later in *Tap Press Read,* edited by Lisa Murphy Lamb (Loft on EIGHTH, 2020).

Contributors

Rona Altrows is an essayist, fiction writer, editor, and playwright. She is the author of three books of short fiction, *A Run on Hose, Key in Lock*, and *At This Juncture*, and the children's book *The River Throws a Tantrum*. She has co-edited two previous University of Alberta Press anthologies, *Shy*, with Naomi K. Lewis, and *Waiting*, with Julie Sedivy. Her ten-minute plays have been produced and published in Canada and the United States. Her honours include the Jon Whyte Memorial Essay Award, the W.O. Mitchell Book Prize, and two Independent Publisher Book Awards (IPPY).

Debbie Bateman is a graduate of the Writer's Studio at Simon Fraser University. She recently completed a collection of linked short stories about women at mid-life and their relationship with their body. The two stories that appear in this anthology will appear in that collection. Her work is in the anthology *Shy* and has appeared or is forthcoming in *descant*, *Euphemism*, and *Emerge 18*. She blogs about creative writing at debbiebateman.ca.

Moni Brar is an Indian-born Canadian writer and poet who explores the intersection of race, culture, and gender and its impact on identity and belonging. She's intrigued by the role of power and privilege in the immigrant experience. Her work has been published in two anthologies—*This Place a Stranger: Canadian Women Travelling Alone* and *Boobs: Women Explore What It Means to Have Breasts*. She is a member of the Writers' Guild of Alberta and the Alexandra Writers'

Centre Society. She was selected for the 2019 Borderlines Writers Circle, an intercultural initiative that serves writers from many linguistic and cultural backgrounds.

Maureen Bush has a BA in History and a Masters degree in Environmental Design (Environmental Science), is trained as a mediator, and no longer does any of these things. She has five novels published for children: *Feather Brain*, *Cursed,* and a trilogy: *The Nexus Ring*, *Crow Boy*, and *The Veil Weavers*. She began meditating when her mother dragged her to a Transcendental Meditation class when she was a teenager, and stopped immediately after. This did, however, set the seed for a later interest in Tibetan Buddhism. Maureen is a long-term meditator and has been deeply changed by the practice. She lives in Calgary.

Sharon Butala is a prize-winning, best-selling author of twenty books with two more on the way, including *This Strange Visible Air: Essays on Aging and the Writing Life*, a collection of essays out in 2022. Her latest is the short-story collection *Season of Fury and Wonder* about the lives and thoughts of old women. She has also had five plays produced, as well as numerous articles and essays and a poetry chapbook. In 2002 she became an Officer in the Order of Canada. She has also been awarded three honorary doctorates and the Saskatchewan Order of Merit.

Jane Cawthorne's most recent publication is the 2017 anthology *Writing Menopause* with E. D. Morin. Together, they also edited *Impact: Women Writing After Concussion*, due in 2021 from University of Alberta Press. Her work has appeared in newspapers, magazines, scholarly journals, literary journals, on the CBC, and in other anthologies. Her roots as a feminist activist go back decades. She writes about women in times of transformation. Her play, *The Abortion Monologues*, has been produced numerous times in Canada and the United States.

Joan Crate taught Creative Writing, English, Children's Literature, and Indigenous Literature for over twenty years. She writes both poetry and fiction, with a bit of academic work thrown in. Over the years she has been shortlisted for, placed in, or won several awards including the Commonwealth Book Award for Canada, the Bliss Carmen Award for poetry, and the W.O. Mitchell award in 2017 for her latest novel, *Black Apple*. She lives in Calgary and spends time in the Okanagan with deer and marmots.

Dora Dueck is the award-winning author of four books of fiction as well as stories, essays, and articles in a variety of journals. Her most recent novel is *All That Belongs* (2019). Her novel *This Hidden Thing* won the McNally Robinson Book of the Year award at the Manitoba Book Awards and was shortlisted for the Margaret Laurence Award for Fiction. *What You Get at Home* won the 2013 High Plains Award for Short Stories, and her novella *Maskwas* was the winning entry in the 2014 Malahat Review novella contest. Dora grew up in Alberta and lived for many years in Winnipeg, but currently makes her home in Delta, British Columbia.

Cecelia Frey lives and writes fiction and poetry in Calgary, Alberta, Canada, the World. She is a lover of old wine and old movies. Her latest novel, *Lovers Fall Back to Earth*, explores the conundrum of the male/female binary. Her latest book of poetry, *North*, explores the existential complexities of being born in a cold climate. In 2018 she received the Writers' Guild of Alberta's Golden Pen Award, given for lifetime achievement of outstanding Alberta writers. Her blog is *The Writing Life*, at ceceliafrey.wordpress.com.

Ariel Gordon is the Winnipeg-based author of two collections of urban-nature poetry, both of which won the Lansdowne Prize for Poetry. Recent projects include the anthology GUSH: *menstrual manifestos for our times*, co-edited with Tanis MacDonald and Rosanna Deerchild, and the fourth installment of the National Poetry Month in the Winnipeg Free Press project. Her most recent book is *Treed: Walking in Canada's Urban Forests* (2019).

Elizabeth Greene has published three books of poetry, *The Iron Shoes*, *Moving*, and *Understories*, and a novel, *A Season Among Psychics*. She edited and contributed to *We Who Can Fly: Poems, Essays and Memories in Honour of Adele Wiseman*, which won the Betty and Morris Aaron Award for Best Scholarship on a Canadian Subject (Jewish Book Award). She selected and introduced *The Dowager Empress: Poems* by Adele Wiseman. Her first career life was teaching English at Queen's University, and she still lives in Kingston, Ontario.

Vivian Hansen has published poetry, creative nonfiction, essays and memoir in Canadian journals and anthologies. "Hundedagene and the Foxtail Phenomenon" was published with Guernica Editions in *Coming Here, Being Here*. "Telling" was published in *Waiting*. Her three full-length books of poetry include *Leylines of My Flesh*, *A Bitter Mood of Clouds*, and *A Tincture of Sunlight*. "Design Charette for Blakiston Park" was published with Loft 112 in 2019. Vivian teaches poetry and creative writing with the University of Calgary.

Joyce Harries lives and writes in Edmonton. She has worked as a florist and a caterer and has run artists' retreats in an Okanagan vineyard. She began writing in 1996 and has since had three books published: *Girdles and Other Harnesses I Have Known*, *Twice in a Blue Moon*, and *A Wise Old Girl's Own Almanac*.

Elizabeth Haynes's fiction and nonfiction have appeared in magazines including *Alberta Views*, *The New Quarterly*, *The Malahat Review*, *Prism*, and *Room*, and in anthologies, including *Waiting*, *Shy*, and *An Anthology to End Violence Against Women*. Her short-fiction collection *Speak Mandarin Not Dialect* was a finalist for the Alberta Literary Awards.

Paula E. Kirman is an award-winning writer, photographer, filmmaker, musician, and activist from Edmonton. She edits an inner-city community newspaper and works with numerous non-profit groups as a communications and media consultant. Some of her awards include the Award of Merit for Advocacy of Social Justice from the Edmonton Social Planning Council, The Salvos Prelorentzos Peace Award from Project Ploughshares Edmonton, and the Human Rights Champion Award from the John Humphrey Centre for Peace and Human Rights for being a pioneering media artist and community organizer. She has also received First Prize in the 2016 Edmonton Inner City Poetry Contest and was a finalist in the 2017 International Songwriting Competition.

Joy Kogawa is an author and activist, best known for her novel *Obasan*, which has been taught in schools and universities across Canada. She has received numerous honorary doctorates, the Order of Canada, the Order of British Columbia, and the Order of the Rising Sun. She presently lives in Toronto.

Laurie MacFayden is an award-winning writer, painter, and sports journalist who has published three poetry titles with Frontenac House. Her writing has also appeared in *The New Quarterly*, *Alberta Views*, *FreeFall*, and *Queering the Way*; and been performed in Edmonton's Loud & Queer Cabaret, the Skirts Afire Festival, and the Queer the Arts Festival in Calgary. Her short story, "Haircut," won the Howard O'Hagan Prize at the 2017 Writers Guild of Alberta Literary Awards, and her debut collection, *White Shirt*, was short-listed for the Lambda Literary Awards.

JoAnn McCaig is the author of two novels, *The Textbook of the Rose* and *An Honest Woman*, as well as the critical study *Reading In: Alice Munro's Archive*. She taught university English for many years and is now the owner of Freehand Books and the co-owner of Shelf Life Books.

Wendy McGrath's most recent novel *Broke City* is the final book in her Santa Rosa Trilogy. Previous novels in the series are *Santa Rosa* and *North East*. Her most recent book of poetry, *A Revision of Forward*, was released in 2015. McGrath works in multiple genres. BOX (CD) 2017 is an adaptation of her long poem into spoken word/experimental jazz/noise by QUARTO & SOUND. MOVEMENT 1 from that CD was nominated for a 2018 Edmonton Music Award (Jazz Recording of the Year). She recently completed a collaborative manuscript of poems inspired by the photography of Danny Miles, drummer for July Talk and Tongue Helmet. Her poetry, fiction, and nonfiction has been widely published. In 2018 her essay "Alterations" from the anthology *Waiting* was nominated for the James H. Gray Award for Short Nonfiction.

E. D. Morin's writing appears most recently in *New Forum*, a new Calgary women's arts and culture magazine. She is the editor of *Writing Menopause: An Anthology of Fiction, Poetry and Nonfiction* with Jane Cawthorne. Together, they also edited *Impact: Women Writing After Concussion*, due in 2021 from University of Alberta Press. E. D. Morin's essays, fiction, poetry, book reviews, and interviews have been published in literary magazines across North America, and her work has been produced for broadcast on CBC Radio. Two of her stories currently reside in the Short Story Dispenser in the new Calgary Central Library.

Lisa Murphy Lamb is author of the novel *Jesus on the Dashboard* and director of Loft 112, where she curates readings, publications, and festivals, and celebrates the literary community in Calgary.

Lorri Neilsen Glenn's nonfiction works include the award-winning *Following the River: Traces of Red River Women*, a mixed-genre exploration of her Métis foremothers; *Untying the Apron: Daughters Remember Mothers of the Fifties* (now in its third printing); and a bricolage essay collection, *Threading Light: Explorations in Poetry and Loss*. Former Halifax Poet Laureate, Lorri is a mentor in the University of King's College MFA program in Creative Nonfiction and the recipient of an award for teaching excellence. Her popular workshops in poetry, nonfiction (including memoir), and manuscript development are offered across Canada. Find her @neilsenglenn

Olyn Ozbick is an internationally award-winning journalist and magazine editor, a finalist in the CBC Short Story Awards, and author of the popular picture book *The Davy Rule*. Her short stories have been published in anthologies and literary magazines in Canada, the US, and the UK. She lives in Calgary with her frisbee-lovin' border collie.

Roberta Rees's writing is described as musical and moving. Her publications include three award-winning books—*Long After Fathers*, *Beneath the Faceless Mountain*, and *Eyes Like Pigeons*—as well as many essays, poems, stories, and a thirty-minute film, *Ethyl Mermaid*. Writing awards include the ReLit Award for Short Fiction, the Canadian Literary Award for Personal Essay, the Canadian Literary Award for Poetry, the Georges Bugnet Award for Fiction, and the League of Canadian Poets' Gerald Lampert Award. In 2019 she won the James H. Gray Award for Short Nonfiction for "Bones, Baby," her essay in *Waiting*.

Julie Sedivy is a writer of nonfiction whose work has appeared in the *Canadian Literary Review*, *Nautilus*, *Discover*, *Scientific American*, and *Politico*. She is the lead author of *Sold on Language: How Advertisers Talk to You and What This Says About You* and the co-editor, together with Rona Altrows, of *Waiting: An Anthology of Essays*. She is currently writing a book about losing and reclaiming a native tongue, to be published by Harvard University Press. Sedivy has taught at Brown University and the University of Calgary, and now makes her home on the beautiful lands of Treaty 7.

Madelaine Shaw-Wong teaches creative writing at the Alexandra Writers' Centre in Calgary, Alberta. There, she is part of a team involved in AWCS's coming fortieth-anniversary anthology. Madelaine is the author of a dystopian novel, *Quietus*. She co-wrote *Cradling the Past*, a biography that is now part of Calgary's Glenbow Museum's permanent collections. She has also published short stories in various journals and anthologies, including *Shy*, *Mused*, and *Dark Gothic Resurrected*. Her website is madelainewong.com.

Anne Sorbie is an author and editor. Her third book, *Falling Backward into Mirrors*, a collection of poetry, was released in 2019. Anne's fiction, poetry, essays, and book reviews have been published by the University of Alberta Press, Frontenac House, House of Blue Skies, and Thistledown Press; in magazines and journals such as *Alberta Views*, *Geist*, and *Other Voices*, and online with Brick Books, CBC *Canada Writes*, and *Wax Poetry and Art*. She is co-editor, with Heidi Grogan, of *The (M)othering Anthology*, to be published in 2022.

Aritha van Herk is the author of five novels, *Judith*, *The Tent Peg*, *No Fixed Address*, *Places Far from Ellesmere*, and *Restlessness*, five works of nonfiction (most notably *Mavericks: An Incorrigible History of Alberta*), two works of place writing (with George Webber), and a work of prose-poetry, *Stampede and the Westness of West*. She has published hundreds of stories, articles, reviews, and essays on Canadian culture, material culture, and women's experience. She is a member of the Order of Canada and the Alberta Order of Excellence. She lives in Calgary, Alberta.

Laura Wershler's writing is grounded in her decades of experience as a sexual and reproductive health advocate, commentator, and educator. Her work has appeared in various newspapers, journals, online media, and the 2016 anthology *Without Apology: Writings on Abortion in Canada*. While earning a certificate in journalism from Mount Royal University (2011), she discovered a love for editing the words of others. She is co-editor of *Musings on Perimenopause: Identity, Experience, Transition*, a collection of scholarly papers, personal narratives, and has poetry scheduled for publication in 2021 by Demeter Press.

Other Titles from University of Alberta Press

Waiting

An Anthology of Essays

RONA ALTROWS & JULIE SEDIVY, *Editors*

This diverse anthology of contemporary creative
nonfiction explores the universal agony and hope
of waiting.

Robert Kroetsch Series

Shy

An Anthology

NAOMI K. LEWIS & RONA ALTROWS, *Editors*

Shyness needs no cure, claim the authors of
thoughtful, raw, and humorous essays and poems.

Robert Kroetsch Series

Impact

Women Writing After Concussion

E. D. MORIN & JANE CAWTHORNE, *Editors*

Twenty-one women writers offer vital counter-
narratives to "one-size-fits-all" descriptions of
traumatic brain injuries and recovery.

More information at uap.ualberta.ca